Heavy is the Head Those Who Wear

The Entrepreneurial Kingdom

Werd Pley Publishing © 2020

www.werdpleypub.wordpress.com/

Copyright © 2020 Werd Pley Publishing and Curtis Florence

All rights reserved.

No parts of this work may be copied without the author's permission.

Contents

Dedications	5
Praise for Heavy is the Head for Those with Crowns	6
Acknowledgements	7
Introduction	8
Chapter 1: Crowns Dripped in Blood	9
Chapter 2: Foundations Built of Bricks	15
Chapter 3: They always come for you	17
Chapter 4: The Top Can Be Lonely	21
Chapter 5: Life Makes You Take a Knee	27
Chapter 6: Live like a legend	30
Chapter 7: King	34
Chapter 8: Protect the squadron	39
Chapter 9: Invisible Scars	44
Chapter 10: Be better than me	48
Chapter 11. Protective Skin	53
Chapter 13: Told you so	58
Chapter 14: Queens	61
Chapter 15: Gladiator School	67
Chapter 16: Don't skip on freedom	71
Chapter 17: Worthy	73
Chapter 18: Moments of Surrealism	77
Chapter 19: Operation Yellow Brick Road	81
Chapter 20: Slide shows	85
Chapter 21. Untamed Spirit	88
Chapter 22 Together	91
Chapter 23: Passing the Mantle	94
Chapter 24. Facades & Castles	99
Chapter 25: Laying the Blueprint	102

Chapter 26. Concrete to Palm trees	104
Chapter 27 Black Excellence	107
Chapter 28: The Royal Chairs	112
Chapter 29: Knighted	115
About the author	118

Dedications

I have written this book for young kings and queens that feel that the world is theirs for the taking. Also, for my mom, Ramona Parnell, and for my best friends, Erica Acevedo, Kettia Green, Trisha Matos, and Janelle Glenn. They have always been there to catch me when I felt I started to stumble. In addition, for my good friend Cindy Leader. She has kept me focused on my goals and has shown unwavering support as I pursued each of my goals. Last, but not least, this book is dedicated to my Grandpa Eddie. He set the standard high as an entrepreneur for himself, and it is his path that I now faithfully follow.

Praise for Heavy is the Head for Those with Crowns

"David is a great friend of mine that I have known for years. I have had the opportunity to watch him grow on many levels. He inspires me every day to be great with his actions. I was very proud to find out he was going to write another book. I believe everyone should live their dreams and be more creative in life. I can't wait to get my copy of David Williams' book. I wish him peace, light, and prosperity." Janelle Glenn ~ Writer/Publicist

"It was really good I enjoyed the first paragraph. A lot of people find themselves in your position and many don't live life and as you state, "Step up." Not many can evolve because they hold themselves back. I'm sure if your whole book follows suit, I can definitely see it helping those in a similar position and bringing their true selves out." Dino Brienza ~ Ironworker

"I think it's perfect!" Erica Acevedo ~ Author/Teacher

"One thing that excites me most about this young entrepreneur and author is that in the short amount of time that I have known David Williams, I have seen clarity develop around his passion for writing. He has created such depth within his books and I have witnessed first-hand his growth as a writer as he has poured his heart and soul into this third book of his, while not only wanting to better himself, David's writing embodies the qualities of a person who has truly dedicated his time wanting to help others grow from his own personal life experiences. Following an inner calling and breaking the norms of society can be scary, and the awareness that comes along with this venture can be confusing. David puts it all out there and wears his heart on his sleeve in *Heavy is the Head for Those Who Wear Crowns*. In turn, his readers will be drawn in and will benefit from his frankness and encouraging words during their own exciting time of following their entrepreneurial dreams."
Cindy Leader ~ Teacher/Editor/Writer

"Read it! Love it! *Heavy is the Head for Those Who Wear Crowns* definitely resonates with me. Some of us just need that push and to realize we deserve what we are seeking, and it's okay to want it." Angela Churchill ~ Marketer

Acknowledgements

Over the years, I have had countless engaging conversations with both alpha men and alpha women. Many of these conversations have gone well into the wee hours of the morning as it was too difficult to stop the explosion of creativity once it had been ignited.

Talking to others about their entrepreneurial ideas is something I've always been passionate about, especially when there's a possibility that us working together could form something even bigger. I believe that within each of us there is a king or queen waiting to be embodied once we adorn our individual crowns with courage.

This book will help you reach down deep within yourself to find your majestic nature and exercise your true potential. Certainly, there will be challenges that arise to greet you, but we must stand boldly up to each challenge, and rise above it. There will be moments of frustration and uncertainty but the way you respond to them will define you and shape your destiny so choose wisely. Whether your goal is to become rich beyond your imagination or rise to new heights in your current field, this book is for you.

My goal with this book is to provide the necessary motivation we all need to cross the threshold of opportunity to see the fruition of our desires.

I thank those who have continued to encourage and push me toward the level that I envisioned for myself. Even though I am the frontrunner of my dreams, I am certainly not a one-man show. I have had plenty of help in advancing toward each of my dreams. Help comes in all shapes and sizes and no matter the source, is always useful. My best advice; never let other people suffocate you with the weight of their own situations.

Live your life, dream big and rise to the occasion. Regardless of whether you are a single mom, single dad, striving to achieve a higher level of education, or even establishing your own corporation, embrace the royalty within and allow it to be a personal beacon as you follow your dreams.

Introduction

The throne of any king or queen must begin in the mind. It is there that you must first take your seat and govern your affairs. A true king or queen will be known by their wise decisions. Many trials and tribulations will come before you and if you rise to the challenge as I have, it will cement your position of leadership.
Some kings and queens choose the path of ruthlessness and some choose to be sincere and genuine. I have chosen the latter as my path in effort to help build others and not burn any bridges behind me. If you can find common ground with others it is very likely that you will help each other advance in life. It seems unlikely, but you do meet other kings and queens along the way who have similar experiences that you both can build from. Throughout my journey I have been fortunate enough to meet others who have helped me build a more solid foundation for my own castle.

Let this book be a blueprint for any king or queen currently rising to their throne. No matter how it may feel, know that you are never alone in your journey. There will be those who try to take your position on the throne instead of preparing their own, but if you are cemented in your position, there will never be a threat to it.
You will be tested from all angles, even those closest to you because they can't see your vision, but that's why it's <u>your vision!</u>

Focus on your destination and never allow yourself to be held back. Once you know where you're going you must also know that you can't take everyone with you. Developing this level of understanding will help strengthen your kingdom and keep you well prepared for life because things can quickly change

Chapter 1: Crowns Dripped in Blood

"Blood reveals the wounds of success."
~ D. Williams

Let me first say congratulations on embracing your inner king or queen! Very few can withstand the pressure that comes along with such a task. A task that can either make or break you. Although daunting, anyone driven to follow their passion in this world must dig deep, dig often, embrace their inner king or queen with confidence and take the first steps on their journey.

What I saw projected for myself was very different from what others saw in me. Deep down I knew exactly what I wanted to do and what I wanted to become, but I was never bold enough to go for it. What little courage I had was fleeting and unseen like a passing summer breeze. In most situations, whatever strength I had usually remained below the surface.

The people around me usually caught glimpses of my potential and what my dreams would become, but their support was just as fleeting as my own courage. I realized that being true to myself was the most important thing I could do to actualize the dream I had buried deep down inside. I ignored my intuitions, dragged my feet, resisted every urge and waffled my decisions long enough, so I knew it was time for my dreams of entrepreneurship to become my prime focus. There was no turning back. Hesitation was now a thing of the past and more importantly there would be no rushing of the process. Armed with the support and guidance of a dear friend my dream started to become evident. I knew that it was time to stand up to the challenges before me, many of which were self-made.

The first step, as usual was the hardest. I left my job and secluded myself in an environment with minimal outside support or distraction. Although scary it was a necessary change to ensure my success.

No longer in denial and having fully stepped into the position of author, along with fragrance entrepreneur and launching my own wine company, the life I envisioned for so long was starting to become a reality. Now it's time to become the king I deserved to be.

Seeing myself as a true king has completely transformed my mindset for better. Initial changes were small but were monumental none-the-less. I began consorting with an entirely different caliber of people that consisted of entrepreneurs and others who were natural go-getters. I changed the music I listened to, the caliber of books I read, and studied business videos. I pretty much immersed myself in the "laptop lifestyle," enabling me to work from virtually any location I traveled to. I loved being able to work from anywhere and my dreams were becoming a reality right before my eyes. The king approaches the throne.

Countless decisions were placed before me that I realized no one else could make, but that comes with the territory. The biggest rule of responsibility; the buck stops with you. The king or queen never delegates their decisions to others.

At times it will feel like there are constant roadblocks and even days when moving forward feels like the wrong choice, but again this comes with the territory. There will be many late nights, and even thoughts of giving up but success comes in its proper time. No matter the circumstances, each challenge is temporary and must be perceived as such. There will be high anticipation, and waiting that seems forever, but fruition takes true patience. In order to become a true king or queen your crown must be earned through blood, sweat, and tears.

The meaning of having a crown dripping in blood is simple – there are battles, there dues, and no matter the outcome, each stripe is earned. Most battles will be internal so you will question your own decisions quite often. For me, it consisted of scattered nights crying myself to sleep, asking the Universe and/or Powers-that-be to keep me focused on my journey to billionaire status. Decisions will be critical on your journey and sometimes it only takes one to open a flood gate of golden opportunities. I have learned to trust my own judgement and not doubt myself or get distracted by outside noise. Those trivial things can pull you in a thousand different directions.

To withstand this, you must be disciplined and at times be willing to sacrifice even your social life. These are some of the dues a king or queen must pay through hard work and endless planning. Real challenges will present themselves, hence, the crown will be dripping with the blood of war. No matter the scars, wear your crown with pride.

In adolescence I always challenged authority. Although I had tremendous potential, a trail of truancy seemed to follow me. Schooled seemed boring to me and I often contemplated quitting, but my mother wouldn't dare let me drop out without finishing the first 12 years at least. Dropping out early was always a huge temptation, especially with so many success stories of drop-out who turned into multi-millionaires.

This was the start of my journey towards my own entrepreneurial crown which would soon be adorned with my own blood, sweat, and tears. I payed my dues by resisting the easy road and staying in school, then continuing to college where I earned a degree in marketing. The internal struggle was the hardest to overcome, but I am forever thankful that I faced it head on.

The most important lesson I have learned on my journey so far is that the real version of you is the inner you and that is what truly matters. A sharp, three-piece suit does not prove a person's level of success. The outer appearance creates a façade that can mislead one's perception as it did my own. Seeing people dressed, with such importance made me feel they had it all, and in most cases, they had nothing more than the suits on their backs. My impression of people wearing suits was so high until I learned a quote that was quite humorous to me; *"You think people who wear suits are successful until you realize they work for people who wear pajamas."*

My takeaway from this is that although every entrepreneur may dress sharply, nothing reveals a person like their own behavior. Behavior brings out the inner person so pay close attention to it. My personal outfit-of-choice is simply a nice buttoned-down shirt with dress pants although I will wear a full suit if needed. The true beauty of entrepreneurship is that there is no set uniform. Your grind is the same whether you work at home or leave, whether you go to a warehouse or Starbucks. Living life by design, however you see fit, is the beauty of entrepreneurship. I've found that there is no manual for being an entrepreneur, or for life in general for that matter, so you will learn a lot on the journey. Trust your gut instincts. This is your personal journey, so be happy and live out your dreams. You will make mistakes along the way, but your growth will be exponential. My advice to you; when it comes to business and finance, always set firm goals, stay on course and never give up.

It was at the age of 25 that I decided to reach for my crown. After working several standard jobs, I realized nothing was fulfilling, nor did they seem to be a good fit. I have also never been comfortable with the idea of being expendable. I soon realized that no matter how much time I invested in someone else's business or project I could be taken out of the equation at the drop of a hat. Questioning everything became the norm, until I made the decision to become an entrepreneur of my own efforts.

At this point in my life, I truly believe that I discovered entrepreneurship when I was supposed to. When I look back, I would have preferred to start my journey a few years earlier, but the Universe leads the way and I follow.

Armed with a new mindset and ready for anything that would be thrown my way, one of the first things I did was to stop comparing myself to others. I noticed I was envious of others who were younger yet had much more success than I had. I realized how toxic it was to always compare myself to others and what I perceived as success. I began to develop pride in my own successes no matter how big or small. I realized the path was mine alone to follow, so I decided to simply be myself and focus on my own path.

Wearing the proverbial crown will leave you vulnerable to the opinions of others who make assumptions on what they see instead of learning the full story. They make focus on the glamour and prestige of your crown or, if they're pessimistic, they may even focus on the wounds and failures of your journey to prove you are unworthy. At some point you must understand that it is not your job to fix other people's perception or constantly explain why this is your vision. Trust me, that will waste a lot of your time and energy.

You will also come across those whose thinking may be a little back dated, who may tell you how you need to be "realistic" and/or get a "real job." Since times change it is important that our way of thinking change with them. When someone uses the term "realistic" to convince me that they know what was best for me, it burns me up inside. It promotes doubt and implies that my hard work is simply futile. I chose to ignore those who berated me with such responses. I was behind the steering wheel of my future and I certainly was not in need of a back-seat driver.

I would never take issue with others giving advice of course, but if the advice hinders me from my goals and dreams then keep it for yourself. I have always leaned on my own independence as much as possible so that I could look back at my own hard work with pride. This is the way I chose for myself. My head, my crown, my blood, sweat, and tears.

Where I have placed myself in the realm of life never ceases to amaze me. Living by my own decisions, my own rules and even allowing my own mistakes makes me feel virtually bulletproof like a superhero. That is by far the best feeling you could ever experience and it's available to anyone who reaches for it. The freedom of running my own business and working from virtually anywhere in the world is a reality that I hope reaches everyone. I live (as the millennials say) the "laptop lifestyle" which means; if there is a wi-fi signal for your phone or laptop, you can work from anywhere. This access has changed my life.

The beautiful thing about this journey is that there are many ways to navigate through it. Think of it like getting into your car with the goal of reaching a certain destination, yet there are several routes you can take to get there. You can choose longer or shorter routes, go fast or slow, have passengers or go alone. Do not allow others to convince you that your choices are limited when you know better.

What makes entrepreneurship so exciting is that you oversee all aspects that run the business. You also know in your heart the people that are fully supportive because they represent the "green lights" on your journey. Once you build up momentum the power and speed may seem intoxicating, but stay focused on your goal, straighten up your crown, and wipe off the occasional blood that comes with the territory.

Chapter 2: Foundations Built of Bricks

"Use the stones people throw at you to build a foundation." - D. Williams

Starting my own business was no easy task; I had to have a strong foundation of ideas as my starting point. In the beginning of my journey I was wary and on edge because I allowed others with strong opinions to get under my skin. I had to realize that there would always be others with their own opinions and ideas, but I'm not obligated to agree with them. I can't control what other people think or what level of support they decide to give. The best thing for me or anyone on their journey is to not rely so heavily on other opinions, but to instead extract the good from the bad. Just remember, opinions are a dime a dozen so invest wisely.

You control the flow of ideas, after all, you have your own ideas to invest in first. In the beginning many others could not understand my line of thinking, but I was determined to follow through and not be deterred. I had my own ideas to build on and I had to make sure my foundation would be a strong for my business to succeed. I needed to follow my own path instead of feeling pressured to please everyone and running myself ragged. I decided to build my own line of businesses comprised of books, fragrances, and unique, flavorful wines. The king takes his crown.

My overall business concept is akin to building the foundation of a home. It takes precise skill, invested time, and careful planning. This way of thinking seemed to come natural to me when it came time to build each of my brands. Some things you just can't rush. Just as blueprints would be drawn to map out a new home, Initial planning is key. Start with a strong foundation and build upwards from there. There is always a step-by-step process to follow so after building my foundation I was ready for the next phase of building my empire. In the same way that you prepare a home I prepared my business. You wouldn't buy furniture before the floors are laid and walls erected. You also wouldn't begin marketing a product that is still in production. A strong foundation is key.

Time is extremely valuable, and when it comes to drawing the blueprints for your business, your foundation must be strong enough to hold everything else up. Careful planning will determine the strength of your foundation, so never allow your business to be built using someone else's blueprints.

I believe wholeheartedly in the transference of energy so I did my best to avoid any advice that would take me and my business in a completely different direction. Quite often people who couldn't comprehend the workings of my brands would rush me towards the completion of them before they were ready. Whenever I allowed people like that to interject my ideas it would always interrupt my progress. These days most people would like to microwave their success, but I believe in the saying; you can't rush perfection. In my opinion; slow and steady wins the race.

I experienced many trials and tribulations and each one has made me who I am today. Over time friends and even some family have come & gone, so I grew to know my own value and who I really am. I also learned over time the proper mixture of "brick and mortar" that were best for my foundation. I laid them in a specific manner that was based on my vision. I also learned that whether things work out or not, they always happen for a reason. When things did not go as expected I viewed those occurrences as blessings in disguise. Any good contractor will tell you that a set of blueprints will always need revisions along the way. Building a business from the ground up is never an easy task, so allow ideas to shift and build accordingly.

Chapter 3: They always come for you

"Beware of the approach"

When you're in a position of power there will always be hunters out for your spot. Their weapons and sneaky tactics will attack you from all angles. Sometimes they appear like garden weeds; as soon as you rid yourself of one, three more show up. I caution you; every fight is not worth your time so pick your battles wisely. Opposition can come from anyone and any direction, coworker, friend or family. The hardest decision I had to make and so will you, is to cut some people off no matter how much it hurts. Keeping people around who will inadvertently take you off your path is detrimental to your success. Some of them may even envy or resent your progress, so their tongues sharpen just to cut you down to their level. People who may have grown up with you will probably feel a way within themselves because of your progress. I slowly realized that their feelings reflect their own progress, not mine. These types are known by many monikers such as naysayers, Debbie downers, and even the more popular term; haters, so stay guarded and focused on your goals.

They say you need tough skin to be successful, but I must admit, early on my skin was soft and easily penetrable. The littlest things used to upset me, but I suppose success is a double-edged sword. I came to realize that I had a long-standing chip on my shoulder that carried over into my adulthood. The slightest comment would set me off because it reminded me of harsh words I endured as a child. I would always quickly lash out in response. My attitude was always; "I'll show them. They can either catch up or keep up." I've never been able to accept rejection very well. I was repeatedly told that something I wanted couldn't be done and I allowed it to get under my skin. It took a while, but I slowly realized that the word "no" does not necessarily mean never; It simply means not right now.

This rule isn't just for entrepreneurs, it applies to everything in life. It took me a while to fully embrace that concept. In my life experience I was always overly confrontational, especially when someone let me down by not sticking to their commitments. That burned me up inside because I was always taught to be a man of principle. I used to get very emotional when someone had a difference of opinion, but I realized that I was oblivious to diverse thinking. My family's upbringing was so deeply embedded within me I assumed everyone else would simply fall in line. Don't make the same mistake I made by resorting to anger and frustration when someone else's thinking doesn't agree with yours. Not everyone will share your values and principles and that is perfectly okay. Don't waste your emotions on something you have no control over. Different opinions come with the territory.

At one time I was obsessed with being in control with everything I worked on. Because of my personality I felt like I needed to be the "one and only" on every task. I realized that life is much better when you just let things work together. I created so much unnecessary stress for myself by not allowing others to help. There was an immense feeling of relief when I realized it was okay to ask for assistance when needed. In the past I felt that no one could handle the task like I could so why bother. I realized you only make things harder on yourself by not allowing outside help. Pride turned out to be my biggest opponent and now that I've grown from it, I realized it could have killed me in a business sense. Pride can be a silent killer that lurks from within your own subconscious thoughts. One of the greatest acts of business you can learn is delegation. Be willing to have people on your side who are strong in areas you may be weak in. Be wary though; betrayal lurks in the shadows of opportunity.

Keeping the circle around you small virtually quells the possibility of betrayal. Although, it is always still a possibility, stay conscious of your surroundings. I learned the hard way because at the time I was a bit gullible. My stress level was high because I always contemplated who was really on my side and who wasn't. I went above and beyond for others, so I always had high expectations from them when it came to loyalty. Unfortunately, the feelings were not always mutually reciprocated. It took a while, but I realized that high expectations can lead to even higher disappointments. Even now, as I grow, I'm still learning not to take things so personally. Each situation, no matter the magnitude, has a lesson to be learned within it.

Another thing I am learning is that people change throughout life. Everyone that starts with you won't always stay with you and those that initially support you may one day come for your spot. People will certainly speak ill of you if given the opportunity, so I chose to combat that by speaking my truth. If I focus on transparency and being completely honest, my words can never be twisted and used against me. Most definitely there is power in the tongue and I use it as wisely as I possibly can. I no longer use it to complain or anything close to it because that would just attract more things to complain about. Instead, I use the power of the tongue to speak life into people even if they don't act accordingly. I realized that being vindictive and speaking ill of others out of retaliation won't get you very far. In fact, it will only make things worse. Like attracts like.

You can never completely prevent negative people or circumstances from your invading your space, so the best thing you can do is prepare yourself to handle it to the best of your abilities. The enemy comes in all shapes and sizes; expected and unexpected. Opposition may be easier to handle when it's a stranger, but what happens when it's someone closest to you? It can come from anyone from trusted friend to mother or father. I can assure you I don't have all the answers, nor do I know why it happens. My objective is always to make sure I'm still standing when the smoke clears.

The sad truth is that it will happen, and it will hurt, so brace yourself. It can be even harder if you're a soft-hearted person. You may experience people who are seasons and some that are reasons. Some people come into your life then they're gone; it becomes like a revolving door. Those are the seasons. Or there may be those who harbor feelings of resentment because of your progress, and that sucks no matter where it comes from, but it's not the end of the world. For every person that opposes you there are just as many that will support you to the fullest. Keep that in mind when you notice those who give you the "side eye" simply for your accomplishments.

The good part is, there are those who find out just how serious you are, so they step back and let you be you. Those are the reasons. They give you motivation to keep going and to be resilient in the face of adversity. You earn the respect of others when they see that you won't easily budge and no longer take bullshit. Some people will be intimidated by your momentum and tell you to calm down or relax. Never calm down unless you see fit. Naysayers need to see that you mean fucking business. Calmness is akin to relaxation and success is akin to hustle, so the choice is clear. Let them see that you don't fuck around. Stick to your guns as they say, no matter how much it hurts to disappoint others.

Chapter 4: The Top Can Be Lonely

"There is plenty of room at the top, so reach for it" - D. Williams

As they say, reach for the top because the bottom is overcrowded. I certainly agree with that statement. At one time I was surrounded by those who had the "crabs in a bucket" mentality, so it was hard to distinguish between them. Sometimes there's so much bullshit going on around me I wish there was a BS meter that would alert you about people who were full of it. That would eliminate so much heartache that comes along with life. I would avoid all BS if I could, but I guess that's just part of the journey of life. We grow from those experiences. We do have a "meter" of sorts. Some say its intuition, some call it energy or vibes, and some call it the inner voice. No matter the title, I say follow it. I have personally avoided so much drama in my life by following that inner voice.

A big part of being successful is being supportive of others as well. Your fight for success is no different from theirs. Remember, there's enough room for everyone to be successful. I personally think it's a beautiful thing to see others succeed, especially those closest to you that have been striving to win at life. I have close friends that have been around for ten years and sometimes I pinch myself at the thought of how long the road has been with them. It's especially weird because many of those friendships came from people who were completely unexpected.

Then, you have those who may not need to be a part of your circle. You must be willing to walk away from those who no longer have your best interest at heart. It's tough but very liberating. It will feel like a tremendous weight has been lifted off your shoulders. Cutting ties with people has always been an area of weakness for me because I'm naturally devoted to those closest to me, but sometimes relationships are temporary for a reason. I no longer get upset about it because I realize it's a necessary part of life.

One of the biggest misconceptions about success is that there is only one "top dog". This couldn't be further from the truth. Remember, to attract more success you must be willing to be supportive of others who are in the same fight. It only takes a couple of seconds to congratulate someone on their progress. Successful people should always be happy for the success of others because the law of attraction goes to work on their behalf. Whatever you put into the universe will find its way back to you magnificd. I am genuinely happy and hopeful for people in my circle who are winning in their life and knowing that my well wishes will always come back to me is an awesome bonus.

At one time it used to bother me to be supportive of others because of my own failures and short comings. Coincidentally, once I began to see my own progress it helped me to embrace the progress of others. It feels so much better just to be happy for others instead of showing animosity or jealousy. I realized that I have too much energy invested in my own endeavors to waste on trying to bring others down. I now stay in my own lane, away from all the smoke and mirrors. I only look over to someone else's lane for motivation to step my own game up. Naturally, it bothers me if, and when someone purposely gets in my lane trying to impose their own views. If I want someone in my lane, I'll make the necessary room for them. When people try to force their opinions on me, I'm always so tempted to yell, SHUT UP!

Of Course, I know nothing beneficial will come from doing that, so I simply move past it. That would be a huge waste of my time and energy, which I need for my own projects. Therefore, I try to focus on just being happy for others no matter the situation. One thing I am always willing to do is lend a helping hand to others, especially those who are serious about what they are doing to advance their own lives. In my experience, a few people reached out to help my cause over the years, so I am always happy to return the favor. I wasn't open to this early on but slowly I learned the value of this as I became an entrepreneur. Now that I've learned so much about entrepreneurship, I love mentoring others about it and about writing as well.

I have always been drawn to people and things that allow me to be my natural self and not feel so tense and withdrawn. If you're like me and you're working hard, making good progress and someone intrudes on you with negative energy, it makes me want to get far away from them. Negative energy annoys me, especially when people have nothing to do except complain. I do my best to keep my distance from people with more problems than solutions. I have my own issues to deal with, so I certainly don't want to add someone else's burden to it.

It is literally impossible to help fix a broken person, especially if they won't attempt to help themselves. I was once broken and I hung around other broken people, so we really couldn't help each other. That's like the blind leading the blind. Changing that part of myself took some time because I have always tried to work through things alone instead of seeking help.

Now that I am repairing my own brokenness, I love helping others. Fortunately, I no longer have what I call "superman syndrome." I call it that because I used to try and swoop in, often-times, forcing my help on those who never wanted it. It took a while, but I have now learned to reserve my help for those who want it. This has been a huge stress reliever because sometimes you never know how heavy a long-standing burden is until you finally put it down. This was a hard habit to break because I'm genuinely a kind, and helpful person to those in need. I always feel the need to help when I see an open opportunity. If I'm in public, seeing a homeless person with their cup or hand out, while others selfishly ignore, I feel the need to acknowledge them.

The best advice I ever heard is that money is an amplifier of who you truly are. So, if you are generous with a little, you will be generous with a lot, and if you're selfish with a little, you will be selfish with a lot. There's a thin line between being selfish and being selfless and sometimes you may not even realize you crossed it. I have come close to crossing that line, fortunately I always had someone around to keep me in check. It's very tempting to cross over to the dark side, but I prefer the light so I will stay selfless. Although we all have some bad deeds, I want to be known more for my good deeds. I do believe in karma, which is the same concept as the law of attraction; what you put out will come back to you. It can be a wonderful thing, except when you are on the receiving end of your own bad karma. This is what makes being at the top lonely to a certain degree. If you burn bridges on the way up, they won't be there on the way down either. Everyone falls from grace at some point. We all have regretful situations that we encounter on the way to the top, and someone will always try to remind you of them to knock you back down. The good thing is everyone loves a good comeback story. First, they love you, then they hate you, then they love you again; it's a vicious circle. Being aware of this helps me stay level-headed and far away from arrogance. I do my best not to allow any success to go to my head, and if I do, those in my circle keep me in check.

I always make it a point to be genuine to everyone I meet, because you never know what personal issues they are already dealing with. I accept people as they are and have always operated this way. I try to always take a warm and calm approach whenever I meet other people. Even in school people always said; "he's so nice" and I never even expected that. I was just a genuinely good person. Because of my kind reputation, people would always come to my defense, even if I didn't ask them to. My gratitude was always immense because I realized they were doing something for me that they weren't obligated to do. I always kept that secure in my memories and that has kept my spirit humble. That's probably why it pains me to see other people become arrogant and allow things to go to their heads, then, suddenly out of nowhere, they lose it all. I intend to stay humble.

I'll be the first to tell you I am not the most religious person, but I do strongly believe that whatever you speak into the universe will come back to you tenfold. No matter how much time it takes, it will happen, so my advice is to watch your words carefully. I also had to learn to watch my choice of words so that others wouldn't take offense, especially now that we live in a world of heightened sensitivity. In my younger days you had more liberty to say things without the assumption that you were degrading someone. Nowadays, before you speak, you must think to yourself whether, or not it's "politically correct." I could go on about that forever, but I digress.

If, and when you make it to the top it will never be that lonely if you treat others with fairness and kindness on your way up. As they say, the same people you meet on your way up will be the same ones you see on your way back down. I always want my journey to be as smooth as possible, but everyone you meet is not always compatible, so a smooth road may start to get a little bumpy. I never allow myself to have ill will or animosity towards others even if things don't work out.

Life is too much of a blessing to carry the burden of anger all the time. I make it a point to treat others the best way possible, because I value my own peace of mind. There is something about being in a place of peace that makes you feel unstoppable. I value my peaceful and quiet life, so of course, if something were to interrupt it, certainly that would rub me the wrong way.

Ironically, that wasn't always the case. At one point I used to love drama because it kept my life busy, obviously for the wrong reason. Thankfully I broke that habit and now live and maintain a peaceful life. A drama-free life is a much better memory than a drama-filled life. It was a slow and gradual lesson for me to learn how to live drama-free, but I eventually made it. The hardest part was the task of reminding myself to do better. The fight within is the toughest one.

On your way to the top, never allow yourself to screw people over, or even worse manipulate others to get yourself there. Sometimes, manipulating others may possibly backfire. They may put you in the wrong direction, or even give you the run around, or even withhold valuable information. My response to myself is usually the same in those situations; "don't worry about it".
The fact is, it happened, and it can't be undone, so there's no benefit in getting upset. You, ignoring and moving past the situation may be taken in a negative way, but your peaceful energy will be protected. As you climb your way to the top, watch the company you keep. Some will attempt to kick your feet right out from under you and some will try to sabotage the very path you walk on.

Chapter 5: Life Makes You Take a Knee

"Humble yourself or life will do it for you" - D. Williams

Life has a funny way of showing you the value of silence, not necessarily to stop you from ever speaking, but it shows you how to be mindful of what you say. When I started out as a new entrepreneur my head was enormous. I thought I knew it all, and even when I didn't, I refused to ask for help, even on social media. I also felt that I had the liberty to say anything I wanted, and even though I do, I'm very mindful of my words now that I know how they affect my life. Early on I felt bulletproof, as if I could withstand anything thrown at me, until I bit off more than I could chew.

In the beginning I couldn't make up my mind on what business I wanted to be in, so I tried to do a little bit of everything. There was affiliate marketing, owning my own sneaker line, or even multi-level marketing, among others. These types of businesses had my mind on greed because of the high dollar earning potential. I thought of nothing more than money, but in the end, I didn't make any because I was doing it for the wrong reason. Greed took over me, so the universe taught me a hard lesson by stopping my cash flow. It was a painful lesson, but still a lesson learned. I was always told that a hard head makes a soft backside, and since I was very hard-headed, I found it to be 100% true. It wasn't that I liked being hard-headed, I just preferred taking advice from those who were in a position that I admired.

When people tried to tell me what I couldn't do, I took it as a personal challenge. I perceived it as someone being in my way that needed to move. I will always be headstrong to some degree because I developed a lot of mental toughness over the years.

One of the hardest lessons for me is knowing that not everyone can come with you on your journey. I guess it's just a part of life because people grow at different rates. I've learned a lot of lessons over the years no matter how long it took. I think the universe walks you slowly and gently, but sometimes we fail to realize it. I'm glad that many lessons came early on, so I didn't have much to lose. They caused me to gain a lot of humility early on, so I learned the power of gratitude. Gratitude and humility become a shield that protects you from the onslaught of negative energy around you. Staying humble allowed me to fly under the radar, basically undetected.

I love the fact that people like Bill Gates and Warren Buffett are worth billions of dollars, yet, looking at them you couldn't tell because their everyday apparel isn't flashy. They don't wear brands like Gucci or Prada or Balenciaga, because they have no interest in being looked at merely for their wardrobe. I'll bet you couldn't tell me what type of car they drive, why? Because they're not seeking everyone else's approval.

In this world, overrun by social media, it is extremely rare to find a person without a car. I'm still a work in progress, but I admire men like them and aspire to get to such a level of humbleness yet make a tremendous impact on the world.

Humility played a major part in my social media presence, or should I say lack thereof. The more time I devote to my business and speaking ventures, the less time I have for social media. Oftentimes we fail to realize how much time we spend on it until one day you log in at 1pm and then you look up and it's already 7pm. It's a double-edged sword.
Things were a lot different before the inception of the internet and social media. People didn't interact quite as often, but when they did it had a much deeper significance. These days the internet helps people connect much more often, but, when you think about it, they don't truly feel connected! Social media has basically given everyone "easy button access" to be inundated with personal information of other people without being around them. Truly a double-edged sword!

In my opinion this allows people to become envious of others, so when they see each other in person, judgement is already brewing. You can tell by someone's facial expression exactly how they feel about you. A person may not say a single word but faces tell the whole story. I do my best to not look at others with judgement or even use something negative about them to help my own success. Being used is not a good feeling and I know this from first-hand experience. It's one of the hardest things to bounce back from, especially if it comes from a family member. If it happens to you, stay strong and keep your head up, or you can end up very bitter like I was. I almost shut out the entire world because of something that happened to me. It's very easy to allow yourself to become cold and distant in response to adversity and I almost did.

Thankfully, my conscience didn't allow me to be so easily swayed. I was able to persevere because I developed a strong backbone over the years and built my confidence.

I often have flashbacks of the person I once was. I didn't realize at the time just how gullible I was because I wanted to fit in so badly. I allowed myself to be mistreated, and it also scarred me because my intentions to be accepted by certain people were always pure. Pay attention to each person's aura because sometimes they may not match up and we sometimes make the mistake of overlooking that just to be accepted. Keep this in mind whether it's a business or personal situation.

Chapter 6: Live like a legend

"Be legendary in all aspects of your life"

If you want your life to be happy, better yet legendary, you can't do it with timid thinking. At one time, I had no aspirations to do big things in life like travel and seeing the world. I couldn't even imagine having better things for myself like multiple homes and cars, but my goals and aspirations are now on a much larger scale. Do I regret making a mind shift? Hell no! My only regret is not doing it sooner. Now, my confidence is through the roof and I love every minute of it. In the beginning I knew I wanted more from life, but I wasn't thinking on a global level. I would literally binge watch other people who had the things I wanted and slowly but surely the wheels started turning.

I was never intimidated by the status of others; I just knew deep down that I wanted to be in business for myself. Early on I got a lot of flak from others, but now that they see that I am steadfast, they have stepped aside. People will always show some form of resistance to your ideas, but if you believe in them wholeheartedly then don't allow your opinion to be swayed. The biggest thing people love about me is also the very thing they hate about me – once my mind is made up it can't be unmade. Although I'm not hard-headed like I once was, I'm still head-strong and firm in my decisions because that is a necessity for any good business owner.

Living a legendary life is something I encourage for everyone and some of the great people I've met through social media have kept me in that mind-frame. I am hooked on that concept and I say it to myself in the mirror every day. "I am legendary". It always feels awesome every time I repeat it.

I was always taught that material things should never be your "why." I slowly realized just how one-dimensional that was, so I made my "why" about people, not things. Aspiring for things like fancy cars and houses can be awesome but let that be that the reward of your otherwise hard work. Of course, I would love to have those things, but I would rather that they be a byproduct of my hard work and doing what I love, instead of being my only aspiration.

Of course, receiving a fancy car as a gift from someone else is out of the ordinary, but I wouldn't be opposed to that, depending on who it comes from. I've seen several internet videos where someone gets surprised with a car that costs more than the average person's house, so since I'm a billionaire in the making, I can't wait to do the same. Over the years I've seen quite a few success stories of people who decided to risk it all and it payed off, so I'm inclined to make the same choice with no regrets.

With leadership comes great responsibility, so I used to shy away from it. Why? Because even though others could see those qualities in me, I couldn't see them in myself. Eventually I did see it, and luckily it was sooner rather than later. Most people are still waiting for someone else to swoop in and rescue them from hardship and that's probably not going to happen. The universe gives us all inspiration and opportunities, so it's our choice whether, or not to take them. Whatever the idea is, I'm always filled with gratitude.

I was always taught to treat others the way I would like to be treated, so I approach everyone with sincerity and kindness. No matter how nice you attempt to be, some people still won't be open to it, but I can always rest knowing I tried my best. I no longer allow myself to feel guilty if people decide not to stick around me; I view it as a lesson, not a loss. Over the years I wasted a lot of energy trying to prove to others that I'm a good person, even though they couldn't see it. Trying to please everyone is the quickest way to drive yourself crazy. That's a lesson I wish I learned a lot sooner.

As I continue to work toward a legendary life and add more to my resume, it makes me reflect on the past. I knew early on that I wanted to be known for more than one thing. When I first decided to jump in the business arena my only problem was that a bunch of ideas pretty much hit me all at one time. It was hard to maintain focus because I was equally passionate about each business endeavor. Over time I realized that putting some things on hold to work on others doesn't mean you are quitting. Sometimes your priorities shift from one thing to another and that's okay as long, as you stay focused. Sometimes you may even have to take a step back to assess and organize everything and that's okay as well. As they say, be stern with your vision, but flexible on how you execute.

Sometimes one dream of yours may lead you to another one. I started off writing books which introduced me to speaking among other things. Wanting to live a legendary life is grand task that will take hard work, but I assure you, it is well worth it. The start of a legendary life and becoming a king or queen is simply realizing that your environment or circumstances do not define you. My grandfather is a great example; his home was in a largely segregated area and he was one of only a few African Americans in the neighborhood. He could have moved away from all the discrimination and injustices, but he stood his ground because he was a man of principle. He had unwavering patience because of the goals and dreams he had for his family. After seeing how he stood on his own principles, that became a driving force in my life.

Outside of my own ambition I'm glad that I inherited some of his traits. That's one of the biggest reasons I strive for a legendary life. The most legendary people are the ones who leave a story behind that others can't stop talking about. Some people try to be well known in life for the sake of fame and some people are tremendous by nature because they want to leave behind a respectable legacy. I choose the latter and because of that, my journey has been well worth the hard work.

I have personally vowed that any important move I make must have my heart in it 100%. The legendary rapper Biggie Smalls once said; ***"only make moves when your heart is in it and live the phrase sky's the limit"***. This song; "Sky's the limit" changed my life and convinced me to do just that; reach for the sky. But the more I reach for it, I'm starting to realize the truth; there is no limit because when you reach what you consider the sky, a new one appears, so keep going.

Thinking outside the box has become the norm for me. I try not to think on an expected level because being legendary means something unexpected always comes up and how you respond is critical. I praise the universe for giving me the ability to be resourceful when others along with myself thought it was over for me.

When difficult situations arise, I often think of my grandpa Eddie, and how legendary he become in his life experiences. Seeing his example inspired me to become legendary as well. When I wrote my first book it gave me that legendary feeling, but I knew one book wasn't enough, so I have continued to transcribe my legacy. In the end I want people to look back at my life and say; "he worked his ass off". One of the greatest feelings to have is when people who never met you can still look at your life example and tell just how passionate you were. When you think of someone like Michael Jordan, most of us have never met him before, but I can easily look at his legacy and say; "he worked his ass off." The fact is, he is unforgettable and that's the legacy I am creating for my own life.

I know that my current career choice is the right one because the feeling that I have never happened in any of my former choices. Sometimes it catches me off guard, but it feels good when I'm in public and someone recognizes me for something I've done. In most cases when that happens, I have already moved on to another project, so I'm not even thinking of the things I've already accomplished. I also love the awesome feeling I get when I realize that someone has been inspired by me and uses my life as an example for them to step their own game up. That keeps me inspired and motivated to work even harder. At this point in my life I live by the principle of "pay it forward" because someone showed me a better way, so I do the same in turn. It's a domino effect.

Chapter 7: King

"If you are going to build a castle, make it your own" D. Williams

I am a lover of hip hop music and when I think of king status there are certain hip hop legends that come to mind. I have always looked up to artists like Jay-Z, P Diddy, T.I., 50 Cent and DJ Khaled. These are a few of my favorites who have reached king status because of their brilliance in entrepreneurship. I studied them all religiously and now I apply their strategies in my own business. One thing they all have in common is early on having the foresight to see exactly what successful position they would be in right now.

There is an innate power in words that most people have not discovered. Because of your belief, you can speak into existence circumstances of your inner desires. As they say; thoughts create things. There is a power beyond our comprehension that governs everything around us. Some call it God, or the universe, or the powers that be. Whatever you decide to call it, just know that it works.

A great example of this power is back in the early 90s, when legendary actor Jim Carrey wrote a check to himself for 10 million dollars and even dated it for Thanksgiving 1995. He kept the check in his wallet where it deteriorated, and before he knew it, a call came in for a movie role that would pay him exactly that amount. Seeing this so many times is what made me aim for billionaire status. The law of attraction has worked amazingly in my life, so each day speak the following powerful affirmations over my life:

- I am successful
- I am a billionaire
- I am determined
- I am attracting like-minded people
- I am passionate about my career
- I am living life on my own terms
- I have a blue Lamborghini Gallardo
- I have a black Mercedes
- I have a beautiful home in Massachusetts
- I have a condo in Philadelphia
- I have an estate in Florida

When it comes to affirmations, those are my personal favorites, but of course you can borrow or reconstruct them for your own use. "I am a billionaire" is my favorite, especially because I already think and feel that way. I have been so clearly focused on my affirmations that some people say "hey billionaire" when they address me on social media. It feels right when I hear that because I know that I'm working like a billionaire and not just speaking empty words. I'm sure some people are being sarcastic when they address me that way but speaking the word "billionaire" over me still contributes to the law of attraction. Always be absolute about what you want because once you speak it into the universe you can't take it back. It is so important to watch what you say and how you say it because the law of attraction is always working whether you know it or not.

It's not a difficult concept but most people complicate things by over thinking and I was once guilty of this myself. At one time I couldn't get anything done because my mind was exhausted and not properly focused. Time flies when you're over thinking. A person can spend all day getting nothing done and not even realize it. I think affirmations are a language of their own and those who understand their importance can relate to that. When I first started sharing my affirmations with others, I received abrupt reactions like; What?

That sort of reaction is understandable because I once had the same one, but now that I understand the power of words it brings a smile to my face to see others speak things into existence. Affirmations are good for everything, including your business, love life and spiritual life. There are many universal laws, but attraction is one of my favorites because it is so evident in my life.

Discussing dreams and visions with others is something I truly love because it motivates me to stick with my own and work even harder. My dream came about after seeing that it was possible through the example of others. At this point in my life I could never go back my old way of thinking. I had a victim mentality and when things got tough, I would usually point the finger at someone else. That kept going until I finally got tired of getting the same results.

By playing the victim I was giving power over my life to others and I finally got tired of it. After a while I realized no one else could change my situation except me. The sooner you get rid of the victim mentality, the more progress you will make in your life. Once you take on a winning mindset you'll never want to go back to your old way of thinking. I've always had a "shoot for the moon" personality, so it would always get under my skin when others would tell me to "take baby steps". This was another double-edged sword because I would get so excited to achieve a goal that I would skip steps, but whatever you skip always catches up with you in the end.

The complete process is meant to build you up and reward you, but when you rush the process you end up with disappointment. The fact is, staying focused on your process yields faster results, so it's well worth it in the end. I love the path I'm on and by taking my time, it allows me to be myself, which always attracts the right people.

Energy moves at its own pace, so I have learned to go with the flow and that keeps my life simplified. I no longer allow myself to be rushed to the finish line. As they say, slow and steady wins the race.

The million-dollar question I always get asked is; what upsets you? My answer is; virtually nothing, because I have learned to control my own emotions. I was always taught that if you let someone upset you, they now have control over you. I often feel that I have an "old soul" because I have always been calm and collected in hectic situations as if I was the wise elder.

Taking on the title of king or queen will always bring with it, bouts of adversity. Some will be mental, and some will be physical, but it all plays a part in who you become. I considered myself a king after my first book and speaking gig. I could feel a shift within myself when I had the chance to motivate young children with my own message. Afterwards I was even approached to be a mentor to some, but unfortunately the timing wasn't right.

Whenever I speak or doing anything that displays my creativity, I never have to explain how passionate I am, it just comes through naturally. That lets me know that this is exactly what I'm supposed to be doing. I've always had a quiet, prepared confidence, so I never felt the need to be outspoken. My confidence is more reserved, so I always found it distasteful when I encountered people who were loud about things but had no substance to their words. It didn't really upset me, especially if I didn't know them, but it raised red flags, so I knew that I should avoid them.

I always prefer to be "clean" when I make moves. What I mean by that is; I like to be seamless and not draw unnecessary attention to my actions. Whatever it is, I want it to be smooth with no hassle, but sometimes in life, things happen that are out of your control. It relieves a ton of stress when you get to the point of just letting things be.

When it comes to being a king, it doesn't mean you're walking around with your chest out and your head in the clouds. Being a king is about confidence and belief in yourself, not about ego and belittling others. Of course, you may have an off day here and there, but it's up to you to make sure they never outweigh your good days.

Life is ever changing and the more you keep yourself aware of this, the less hard-hitting it will be when things happen. Sometimes you just need to take a step back and allow yourself to breathe so you can think clearly. Sometimes a person may have multiple dreams that all seem to manifest at once and that can be overwhelming. It's enough to make you want to pull your hair out. I have learned to simply be in the moment with keen focus while still anticipating the reward of the future. As I speak a king's life into existence, I keep myself aware of the fact that I am still going through it. I believe that I already possess a few qualities needed for kingship but others I am still developing. I have always been taught that a king should be humble before anything else, and those who abuse their power fall from grace very quickly. I consider myself humble, yet confident in my position, and anyone who knows me would vouch for that.

I know in the back of my mind that although I have people cheering me on throughout my journey, there could also sometimes be the awkward silence with crickets in the background. Because of this I never take anything for granted. I feel that if your confident in your ability, you can move like a calm wind and still get things done. I usually take the modest approach to things because I refuse to walk around with an air about myself. Some people may misunderstand when you call yourself a king and think you're being arrogant, but this couldn't be further from the truth. Titles like king, queen, empress, and emperor are no different from CEO or President; they're just titles. Judge a person by their actions not their title. There will also be people who believe you don't deserve your position but let that be no concern of yours. Their opinion is their burden because it only holds them back, not you. The title you earn and the time you invest to get there is yours and can't be taken away from you. As the saying goes, we all get 24 hours in a day and time is valuable, so make sure your time is not wasted or stolen by someone else. There's nothing worse than wasted time. A king or queen is always aware of how their time is delegated and they think ten steps ahead of everyone else. It took me a while to catch on to this simple strategy, but it has helped me tremendously in time management. I have also learned the importance of doing things for a valid reason and not just to be "cool" or be part of the "in crowd". When you rise above this level of thinking you're able to say; "fuck the in crowd" and do your own thing. It's a great feeling when you can choose who you want to associate with.

Chapter 8: Protect the squadron

"Quality friendships always beat those of quantity" D. Williams

As an entrepreneur I love the community have become a part of. Some of them have even become like family to me. We can relate to each other when it comes to working late nights or decision making when your uncertain, but I'm sure that happens in other professions as well.
Now that I have worked my way up to higher levels of entrepreneurship, people no longer give me a hard time, but in the beginning, it came from every direction. They would always question; what I did for a living, how long something took me, how I found this path, etc. Initially I would respond with; "none of your business" or "don't worry about it".

I have always been fiercely protective of my products and the amount of energy I put into them. For a long time, I felt that if a person wasn't helping me, they shouldn't be worried about what I do or how I am doing it.
Finding a group of likeminded people, whether online or in person, has allowed me to be transparent about my vision and my passions with this close-knit group. I love being able to share my vision with those who think like I do, on such a colossal scale. For people outside of that circle, it is like prying teeth open just to get me to share information. I love the freedom to do what I want, when I want, and entrepreneurship gives me that option. This way of life has allowed me to escape the "9 to 5" grind and being a slave to the time clock.

I always knew that if I wanted to be happy, I needed a way out of my 9 to 5. My problem was that I looked for others to give me that way out. The friends that I've made as an entrepreneur have become part of my everyday conglomerate. I've known many of these awesome people close to ten years. Over time I have shed many tears because so many people have come and gone, and many of them I wanted to stay around. Although I wanted them to stay, I understand the universe has higher plans, so I appreciate those who did stay.

Since my friends are busy building their own dreams like I am, we don't get to talk every day. We all play the same game but in different arenas. Some of them are in music, some blog, and some write books like I do, but that's the beauty of having a variety of friends. In my opinion, having each of my friends in the same field would be boring because we as people need variety in our lives. I'm sure that if we all wrote books, each story would be different, but we wouldn't have much to discuss. Since I'm more of a laid back and calm person, simple things like books or perfumes work perfect for me. As a naturally calm person, I usually attract people with high energy, so in a way, we balance each other out, and we respect each other's space.

The fact that we respect each other's space and time doesn't mean there is tension between us, we simply have different paths and different schedules. We still interact whenever we can and that works perfectly for us. Some of these friends have gone through the fire with me even before all this came to fruition, so they are cemented in my life. I have been able to do the same for others as well because I gave them my word that I would be there for them and my word is my bond. Anyone around me knows that I say what I mean, and I mean what I say, so if I say it, that's a check you can cash. That's an example of the way I was raised; I am a man of principle and loyalty. I do my best to avoid fickle and disloyal people, in fact years ago I was so bad about it, I was pretty much an asshole. The moment I felt I was being lied to or misled, I would cut people off without hesitation. I don't like to waste another person's time and I certainly don't like my own time wasted. I used to be so paranoid that I wouldn't be able to distinguish between real and fake people, my reaction was to just walk away. It took me a while to scale back my attitude, but I finally learned to be more considerate of the other person's perspective. Because I have started taking my time and paying close attention, I have avoided many potholes that could have made me stumble.

I have gotten to a point where I will follow my intuition before I follow other people. I always felt that following the wrong people would lead me in the wrong direction, so I always kept a back-up plan.

I have a great deal of respect for my close friends because they softened my heart and helped me realize that there are people who will accept me for my true self. I am at my best when I can be authentic and not feel the need to hide behind a mask. When I was younger, I always felt that my creativity was stifled because society gave me the great advice to just "grow up". I guess dreaming of a bigger life than a standard job made no sense. That's probably why my ideas are so abundant now that I have escaped that mentality.

I believe that certain experiences are planned out specifically for us by the universe to help us grow. This concept is something society may not understand, so I have always walked away from those who have no vision for the future. I've always been a lone wolf and have never had a problem staying that way until the right people come along. Walking away from people who expected me to compromise my vision has never been a problem for me. If we could find a compromise between each other sure, but if you expect me to completely stop my dreams I walk away. It's not that I can't work with others, I'm just very picky about the energy I keep around me. Being an empath and a person who is in tune with their self, I stay away from bad energy, mainly those who complain a lot. I mainly avoid them because I have the tendency to get so upset when they whine, I'm bound to just say shut up. It's not that I'm trying to be an asshole, but I have a low tolerance for things that break my concentration or pollute my energy. I can't perform at my best if I'm dealing with your repetitive complaining. It's understandable when a person just wants to tell a story about bad experiences, but once you get overly repetitive it becomes complaining.

When it comes to getting things done, I always do whatever I promise even if it takes a longer time to do it. We live in such a microwave society, so people want things when they think they should have them and if it doesn't happen that way, they quickly lose patience. I get things done without compromising time because I don't follow the microwave mentality. I take the necessary time to get it right. This is the reason my friendships have stood the test of time. They allow me to go with the flow and accept my intentions wholeheartedly. Sometimes we even go months without talking, but when we finally connect it's as if no time has passed.

If I've learned anything from my experience, it's that talking to people every day doesn't prove loyalty. You may not see a person more than once a year and still know that they are truly loyal. There are people I talked to every day at one time and these days we no longer speak.

The best thing about having a conglomerate, even if it is small, is that sometimes your paths cross seamlessly. I have a friend who is a teacher, as well as an author, who shared her vision with me of opening a lounge. Since I'm already building my own lifestyle brands, I realized that it was something we could work on together. I was more than happy to let her take the lead and I could still be a cofounder that just handled the tech stuff. I have another friend who is a teacher that has a passion for investing in stocks. She clearly knows the business well and whatever she recommends I take notes. This is the great thing about having a variety of friends who are strong in areas you may be weak in. It took a while for me to build my conglomerate, but it was worth the wait. I came close to losing faith at times, but my good friends always help rejuvenate me.

Since my conglomerate is made up of others who want an abundance of wealth like I do, it makes it easier for us to hold each other accountable in our goals, whether big or small. It works out perfectly; sometimes I may help them think bigger and they may help me organize my goals better. It's a win-win situation. We complement each other very well. Some of our ideas intertwine and we become a one-two punch to any situation we take on. They catch my blind spots and show me things I don't even notice may **hinder** my success. I must admit, since I'm hard at work and focused, sometimes I miss things, so my conglomerate keeps me on my toes.

These are the reasons that it doesn't matter where I am, even if I'm halfway around the world, if one of them calls I answer. They have put in time with me and I gladly afford them some of my resources as well. I have made a personal vow to share my resources as long, as they are used and not wasted.

I've never been one to need many friends, I'm perfectly fine with 2 or 3 as long, as I know they're sincere. This holds true even to this day. I only have 3 to 4 people currently, that I really confide in. Your circle is a lot easier to manage when it's small. You typically don't have to worry about who's truthful and who isn't because you know them well. I look at it like pulling a wagon full of people. Regardless of the number of people being pulled, they should be helpful, not adding more weight to make the ride harder.

Even though it pained me to do it, I have removed people from my wagon in the past. My goal is to move forward and anyone who intentionally prevents me from doing so doesn't deserve to be a part of my journey. Entrepreneurship is hard enough as it is, so anyone adding more burden to the wagon must go.

In the world of entrepreneurship there is a saying; "being broke is hard and being wealthy is hard, so pick your hard". Because of this I focus on being around those who are progressive and persistent. Seeing people fuel their rockets and soar makes me want to fuel my own and soar to the highest places. I never realized the importance of the people around you until I learned that you are the average of the 4 or 5 people you spend the most time around.

I am grateful that my conversations are no longer about smallminded things, instead I speak of bigger things like owning land or traveling the world. I've gotten to the point that I no longer argue over petty things. I'm much more interested in building for the long term. When it comes to relationships with those who I consider brothers and sisters, I think in terms of time more than anything else.

Chapter 9: Invisible Scars

"It doesn't matter how closely people look some wounds cannot be seen"

As you travel the road to your success there will be some experiences that will leave you scarred. Often times society will tell you to just "get over it", but that isn't always a simple task. Some scars eventually heal, but some are so deep that they linger around as an ugly reminder. The important thing is to not let an old scar taint you or blur your vision. I was almost a victim of blurred vision because I constantly sought the approval of others instead of trusting my own intuition. I asked for help so much that I became dependent on their stamp of approval. I have now learned to trust my own intuition and avoid repetitive, unnecessary drama. Following my own intuition has been some of the best advice I've ever received.

I have never understood why some people enjoy being loud and confrontational. They seem to yell just for the sake of yelling. I find such behavior to be off putting and unnecessary. It's enough to make you want to respond alike, but I just laugh and walk away, especially when I realize how small of a matter they were upset about.

I've always been a cool, calm, and collected person, so it upsets some people when I don't have an explosive reaction to negativity. I really don't care who doesn't like it, what you see is what you get when it comes to me. Refusing to match negative energy can sometimes be dangerous as well because it makes some people even more explosive when you remain calm. Mental toughness is necessary in order to protect your own energy.

Aside from the great money-making potential that comes along with entrepreneurship, I was able to find freedom of expression. Before that, I felt trapped emotionally because I was surrounded by people I could not relate to. My thoughts and ideas had no outlet in the midst of small-minded people. I looked around at my coworkers at the time, realizing just how miserable their lives were and I immediately promised myself, that would never be my life. Seeing them put a little fear in me. It's not that I fear any person, I fear a life of regret. A life stuck in a never-ending loop of normalcy and just getting by. I use that as my personal motivation to keep reaching for the stars instead of staying low to the ground as others would have preferred. I only follow the advice of those who have reached plateaus that I aim to reach and one day surpass. I never follow anyone just for the sake of being a follower.

When it comes to battle scars some can't be completely healed no matter how much we try. Eventually you learn to live with them. I'm proud of my scars, they show that I've fought some tough battles and still survived. It also let's others know that I'm a seasoned veteran in the war we all fight.
My feet are firmly planted because I was always taught that every serious path you take should have at least a ten-year commitment.

I'm glad I took my time and found the best path for myself. I always look at the example of people like Jay Z who started his journey at age 26 and was already a millionaire by age 30. That lets me know that what I'm doing and the goals I have are attainable.

I remember the day I realized I wanted to be a billionaire. I was told it was too big of a goal and that I wasn't even a millionaire yet. Never-the-less, I still shoot for the stars and people around me can either be a part of the journey or step aside while I gas up my rocket.
Either way I'm not staying beneath the grass any longer than I must. This level of zeal has gotten me where I am today, especially since I no longer make decisions under emotional stress. I follow my "spider-sense" more often and my decisions have increased my success tremendously. Better decisions have allowed me to fly below the radar and avoid unnecessary attention on myself.

Although, I have expensive taste, I see why most millionaires and billionaires dress very casually, despite having luxurious cars. I've always felt that things of that nature would be rewards for my hard work and not be the "why" for doing it. My motto is "shut up and get to work" so I do that instead of bringing a lot of attention to myself. In the past I made the mistake of sharing big dreams with the wrong people and it came back to bite me in the ass. If I tell a person I hope to have a mansion or nice luxurious cars, why is it, they feel the need to be judgmental?

It seems that even if you have good intentions for sharing information like that, there will always be someone who will find a way to twist your words around to validate their own judgement. This is the type of experience that can leave you scarred because the judgement may come from those closest to you; friends as well as family. It feels like a stab through the heart that never completely heals. Even if you get past it, there will always be the physical reminder of how tough a situation it was. It may even cause you to question yourself or your judgement, but don't allow that. The truth is, if another person doesn't see your value, it's their loss, not yours. If you try to force others to see that you are genuine it never goes well. Their estimation of your sincerity should come naturally, not by force.

Invisible scars are part of life and should be embraced as such. Despite, the fact that some scars are inevitable, you always have the choice to let them build you up and make you better or tear you down and make you bitter. Just remember, nothing is set in stone, so you can always change your outlook on life. I used to let scars traumatize me and make me bitter, until I concluded that most of them were self-inflicted.

After the matter has passed, the other person that you're upset with us no longer even think about you. Once I realized this, it helped me drop a ton of mental baggage. After dropping the baggage many scars healed a lot quicker.

A lot of the baggage came in the form of those who lurk with no good intentions as well as spectators who hang around like an audience but never offer any support. If you're doing big things and the people around you aren't happy about that, then you need new people. I'm not saying get cheerleaders or yes men, but they should at least be happy when you win. Only recently, I learned to do this on my own and not be so tough on myself. It's up to us to be our own biggest fan.

When it comes to success, most people would tell you to enjoy the process, but sometimes it's not that simple. I can only speak for myself, but sometimes being on the road of frustration feels like a never-ending place. You can see that progress is being made, but not as fast as you would like. When that happens to me, I now take a step back and remind myself that I have achieved more than most people my age. It often doesn't feel like work though because I love what I do.

Chapter 10: Be better than me

"Don't be like me, be better than me"
D. Williams

I love how ambitious I am and most people around me recognize it as well. My mom is one of my biggest supporters, so she loves how ambitious I am. One of the greatest things I learned from her is her supreme work ethic. I couldn't help but notice the excellent blueprint shade laid for me. No matter how hard she worked, I remember when she was in need and humbly asked for help and still couldn't get It. As much of an independent person that she was, it should have been given to her twice over. I remember when she took me to her job so I could see what the corporate world was like and it was a very humbling experience. It had a bigger influence on me than my mother even realized. It taught me that I had to work hard because nothing would simply be given to me. Don't get me wrong, I did get spoiled to a small degree, but most things I certainly had to work for.

My mother used to always encourage me to be better than her, but for the life of me, I couldn't figure out what she meant by that. Now that I've grown and carved out my own path it makes perfect sense.
I noticed that my mom, grandpa and those who came before me all had high standards and confidence levels to match.

Early on, there were things about my mom I didn't like, but one day someone pulled me to the side and they explained to me that when I'm out in the world I'm a reflection of her whether I like it or not. After that it was a lot easier to see where she was coming from, especially since I look just like a lighter version of her.
I wasn't always driven by legacy but the idea of building one eventually caught up with me as I grew older. My grandfather played a huge role in my choice to become an entrepreneur. I was pretty much pushed into this way of life, but it worked out perfectly. I always knew I wanted to help people, but I wasn't sure how I would do it. Now that I have written books and started speaking to groups to spread my message, the path has been made clear.

When it comes to spirituality, I have always believed in God or a higher power, but I never really followed the concept of a specific religion. I am very proud of the person that I've become and even as a child I was told that great things would be in my future. Now that I see things manifesting in my life, sometimes it brings me to tears, because I never expected to be a speaker, let alone running my own businesses.

Being told that great things would happen for me was intimidating, especially since u didn't see myself the way others saw me. I didn't see my potential until I reached the age of 25.

They say the wealthiest place on Earth is the graveyard, and that is because so many people die and take their million-dollar ideas with them. We all have valuable ideas within us, but if we deny ourselves the opportunity to bring them to fruition, they die with us. I refuse to let my dreams follow me to the grave.

I had a bit of a late start, but I'm quickly catching up. I'm proud to be a person who realized their dreams at an earlier age than most. I hear about people all the time who had "so much potential" but never did anything with it. I refuse to be one of those people.

I used to hear people say if you don't put in the time to live your own dreams, you'll spend the rest of your life devoted to someone else's. I'm glad I turned out okay, because my mom stayed on me about maintaining certain values. She's part of the reason that I have high standards and still came out as a good person at the same time.

I still remember when I wanted to do both work and school at the same time, but my mom wanted me to focus on school instead. I was so frustrated because I really wanted to work, but now that I've learned to self-educate myself, I see why she pushed me in that direction. I don't think my mom could have foreseen what I would become later in life, then again, she believed in me 100%, so maybe she did. I hear so many stories about kids who grow up to become successful after their parents die. I'm glad that I was able to start my path to success while my mom is still here.
Even though I was very stubborn as a child, it worked out for my adult life because once I set my eyes on something, there's no turning back.

My mom knew I was ambitious, but she never knew that I wanted to become a billionaire, in fact, I didn't tell her until I was already walking this path. I needed to be certain before I revealed such a lofty goal because I had changed my mind about so many other things. I'm glad that I finally found something to stick with. The best part about it was that my mom was supportive and didn't rush my process. I went from being super defiant to someone who motivates kids, which always makes me laugh because school was not my thing. I'm glad that I finally found a mentor in this field who showed me the ropes. Not that I would never find my way, but it helped the process speed up tremendously.

One thing I've learned is that pride is a killer of dreams, and a silent killer at that. Because of pride I've come close to losing good people in my life, in both business and personal relationships. Pride is also the reason my mom and I didn't always see eye to eye. I never wanted to admit I was wrong, but I've done my best to make up for it and I make sure to thank her every chance I get. My mom always believed in whatever I did, and she never tried to dissuade me. Her focus was always for me to find something and stick with it. These days, to hear my mom say positive things about me is a great feeling. I'm glad she doesn't have to speak about me being ungrateful like many other parents about their own children.

When I think back, I believe that I was drawn to this path because it's a constant learning experience and on top of that, entrepreneurship has so many directions you can take. The possibilities are endless.

I've always been drawn to things that allow you to be yourself. I've never been one to be a follower, but I don't mind taking a backseat until I figure out the proper direction for myself. With certain things that are simplistic I'm usually anxious to take initiative right away, but if the situation is more complex, I take a step back and observe until I'm comfortable enough to act. I am more of a visual learner so I like to be around those I can observe. If I watch someone long enough, I can usually absorb the basics and take it from there.

Success is such a rush, that sometimes I take a step back and pinch myself as a reminder that my dream is now a reality. It happened so seamlessly, that I didn't even notice the transition. In the beginning when I chose to be an entrepreneur, it was very scary because I'm the type of person who loves options. I felt that if I bet it all on this one thing, I wouldn't have anything else to fall back on.

When I first entered the game as a rookie, I didn't have any options, so I was eager to prove myself to everyone else. At the same time, I vowed to myself that my financial status would not stop there.

Now that I am firmly planted in my position, I'm addicted to ownership and I am no longer the "please pick me" person, with desperation written all over my face. Because there was someone to show me the importance of ownership, that is now the primary message I promote in my life.

Never have I been so dedicated to something that is so much bigger than me. It feels amazing to have carved a mark for myself in my family's lineage.

Believe it or not, when I was younger it was flattering to be considered a human garbage disposal because I would eat just about anything. Even though it didn't bother me, I still wanted to be known for more than just my eating ability. I wanted my mom to see more from me and I knew talking wasn't enough, I had to show and prove. To hear her say how proud of me she is and how much of a great young man I turned out to be, means more than any of my accomplishments.

It has been quite the adventure becoming the person that I am today, but I wouldn't have it any other way. There is a lot more in my future, but I'm glad my mom has been able to witness my early successes. She was there to see my first book, my first speaking engagement, and my very first fragrance. That meant the world to me.

It feels like a musician's first Grammy award win. While they're on stage giving their speech, the family is in the audience to witness this epic moment. Even though I haven't been on a stage of that magnitude yet, she has seen me speak behind a podium and at local schools.

I always make sure to show my mom appreciation for her endless effort and sacrifices over the years. It's important to me that she knows just how much of an impact she made on my life. I still have "hardheaded" moments, but she is one of the rare few I would listen to no matter how old I am. Often she would warn me of things ahead of time, but I was too stubborn to listen, then, reluctantly, I would have to admit she was right. Admitting wrong was never an issue for me, but she would hold it over my head for a long time, like "kicking a dead horse" as they say. It bothers me when she, or anyone else does that to me, so in my brain I'm constantly yelling; "shut up" whenever it happens.

My mom always carried herself in a dignified, auspicious manner and she encouraged me to do the same. Granted, she doesn't have the same billionaire goal that I have, but she is complimented as such everywhere she goes. When it came to representing myself with dignity and class I was a bit of a late bloomer, but my mom's message eventually rubbed off on me. I finally realized; to be a billionaire you must think and dress with class. My mom is due tremendous credit because she always worked hard to instill this mentality in me throughout my entire life. She taught me the importance of dressing with color coordination because a respectful appearance is all about presentation. You never know if you're going to be approached by someone who could change your life. At times, I wish that I learned this lesson a lot sooner, but everything happens in due time. Although it took a while, I learned my lesson the hard way as sort of an atonement for my own stubbornness. It turned out to be a valuable lesson indeed. A well-respected man should always dress sharp, whether wearing a suit and tie, or t-shirt and jeans. One should never walk around with a sloppy appearance because your look says a lot about you. Message received. Thanks mom.

Chapter 11. Protective Skin

"Before you step into the world, bring your armor" D. Williams

Although emotions are part of our human nature, it seems that the higher you go in the corporate world, you must take your emotions out of the equation. Perhaps the old saying is true; business is business. Frankly speaking, the higher your achievements, the tougher your skin must be. I've noticed that when failures happen in the business world, you're encouraged to quickly move on and not think twice about it. That's easier said than done for some of us and I can attest to that. I believe that no matter how tough the persona, deep down we are all sensitive to some degree. Ironically, I have been accused of having very little emotion in the past. Frankly, that's not really the case, my emotions are just very guarded. Since I always express myself from a genuine place, I only share them with people who truly understand me. I tend to avoid those who make it difficult for me to express my true self.

In my opinion, if something is already simple it should stay that way instead of complicating and over thinking everything. I know what type of energy I bring to the table, so, if the person on the other end is being anything less than truthful, I have no problem walking away. Having a business career has always taught me to stay on my toes.

Early on, my attitude was; "I do what I want, when I want, and not when someone else tells me to". I have, however learned that everyone must follow someone else's lead to some degree. Even in the world of entrepreneurship there are still plenty of rules to follow. They're a bit different from the rules that are used by corporate America, they still apply just the same. One rule that applies in both areas is that there is always a gatekeeper or "overseer". No matter how much freedom you have in your business, there's always a limit. There's always either a set of rules that limit you or another person or group that governs your situation.

The hard part is when you must be the "gatekeeper" and enforce the rules without room for creativity or spontaneity. In that case you have no one to fall back on. There's no overseer to check behind your work for mistakes or to make sure you met your quota. The fact is; if you're the "overseer" and something falls short, that means you just didn't hustle hard enough. To be in such a lofty position you must make every moment of time and every dollar count as if you won't make another dollar for the next 3 months.

I always credit entrepreneurship with helping me mature and regulating my spending. Before that I was wasteful and had no money management skills. At one point, even if I had 25 cents, I was sure to spend it. I think that my excessive spending was a cry for help. I think I was subconsciously looking for someone to teach me money management. Eventually I realized that I had to take the initiative to teach myself financial basics, and it paid off.

Now that I have learned more about investing and building wealth, my money has purpose. I love this feeling I have, of financial freedom and knowing that my money now has a stronger foundation to build on. I was always taught to save money for a rainy day and my biggest regret is not listening sooner. I'm just glad that I realized it's never too late to start a new habit. The fact is; it doesn't matter when you start, as long as you start. In the beginning I had a terrible habit of starting something and never finishing it. I'm glad I changed my ways, because I never want my reputation to be known for that.

As a person with many layers, each layer sparked curiosity, so it was crucial for me to explore each layer. I've always shown different layers to different people, but I'm glad the layer of toughness is finally starting to emerge.
My personality already has many layers to it; determined, ambitious, sarcastic, visionary, deep thinker, etc. so the only thing missing was a layer of tough skin to protect me from botheration.
Entrepreneurship has toughened me up, so that I can better handle things when someone lets me down because they're unavailable or that something has suddenly come up. I shifted my thinking to now give people the benefit of the doubt instead of assuming the other person is full of shit. No doesn't necessarily mean never, it simply means not right now, so try again later. Hearing "no" still sucks none the less, but you learn to not give it so much power. That one, simple word can be devastating to your heart and mind if you don't understand it's true nature. Everyone's heart is different, and the challenge of rejection is simply a matter of perception. As the old saying goes: "adversity introduces a man to himself".

What is a broken shield? It's a metaphor that means you have been physically or mentally defeated. I've hardly been in any physical fights or altercations in my life, but I have been challenged mentally though. Sometimes people think you're moving too slow or that you can't handle something. These are the types of things that put cracks in your "shield." My shield has had a few cracks over the years; some I was unable to repair.
Having a trusted person to talk to is invaluable in these situations. In my opinion words are everything! They can either make you or break you. Words can help you manifest an awesome life or a nightmare of an experience. Whatever it may be, the perfect life takes time to build.

I've been mentally broken before and after feeling this way for a long time, I vowed that I would never allow anyone to make me feel that way again. Whenever someone attempts to bring me down, I immediately preoccupy myself with something else more important. I am often told that I do too much, but in my opinion, I don't do half as much as I should. I say that because usually when my "shield" had been damaged I kept it to myself. Honestly, I was afraid to admit that I needed help because my trust was shattered to pieces from past experiences. This, of course, was no one's fault outside of my own and I can admit, that is why people tend to distance themselves from me. You shouldn't ask for help and then show skepticism, but unfortunately, that's just what I would do. Fortunately, I have learned to accept help from others without bias and to be thankful for their efforts. Remember; no one is obligated to help you. Help is a choice and is usually born of sacrifice. We must realize that the world doesn't revolve around us and the quicker we get to that point, the better. My shield has been broken and repaired many times, but I realize that this is a part of life that must be dealt with. It takes a long time get your shield back to full strength and mine gets a little stronger each time I tackle adversity. My shield has had its share of scratches and dents which are very visible, but I've strengthened it enough to more than serve its purpose. On the contrary; it not only protects me in daily battles, I've grown stronger as a result. I have no regrets about being broken because it made me more aware of my surroundings. In fact, the cracks in my shield are symbolic. They are a beautiful reminder of my journey as a creative person. My journey has been complex; I've dealt with liars, leeches, businesses I reached out to but never heard back, and people who stood me up. I've also come close to being used by people who meant the world to me. Experiences like those made me numb, especially since those were the people that I used to fight tooth and nail to keep around.

Eventually it gave me a sense of paranoia that someone I trusted would turn on me. Since my journey has been so turbulent, I've gotten to the point of asking people upfront whether they are going to stick around or not. This is mainly because I've been in too many situations where someone promised to do something for me and never followed through. This has caused me to adopt the "I'll do it myself" mentality with other people. Why wait for others when I can just do it myself. It's been rough, realizing that not everyone can be trusted, even if you give them the benefit of the doubt. It's frustrating and I hate operating in this mind frame, but I feel like I had no choice after being disappointed so many times in the past. It made me refuse to wait on others to announce opportunities to me. Instead, I do my best to put myself in position for things to happen.

In business, there's always some sort of adversity in your path. The truth is; the dents in my armor have come from some hard blows. Metaphorically I've been punched in the head, kicked in the stomach, slashed across the face, given a black eye, and had my armor fall off unexpectedly. I've felt like I was stuck and felt like I was moving too slow. These are the types of metaphorical blows that go straight to the heart and I wear the scars like a badge of honor. I'm well aware that my journey will not get any easier, but the fact is, I always love a good challenge. If it were too easy, I would probably get bored and complacent.

I have a bit of a cement head, so I sometimes do things the hard way, but this is only if it's something that I believe in wholeheartedly. In these situations, I often think of a quote from one of my favorite heroes; Captain America;

"When faced with overwhelming odds and when the world asks you to move, it is your job to plant your feet beside the fountain of truth and tell the world NO... you move".

This echoing quote has gotten me through some of my darkest times. Whenever I am about to throw in the towel, I always come across it and it gives me a sense of hope. Despite dark days, and wondering what I should do, I have been able to achieve a lot in a short amount of time. Honestly, it often doesn't feel this way because I am always looking for my next accomplishment to see what else I'm capable of doing.

There's an old saying; "life is short" that I've never cared for because I think it creates a false sense of rushing. It makes you feel that you need to cram everything that you want to do into a small amount of time. Although the pressure is self-applied, the amount of it is overwhelming, therefore hard to ignore.
When it comes to getting things done, I have always been level-headed enough to do full surveillance on something that I am not familiar with. The rare few times that I allowed myself to be rushed, it always blew up in my face, so I fight extremely hard against it.

I typically don't do things the same way others would, but there is a method to my madness. Some people naturally understand my ways but sometimes it gets frustrating to explain it to others, especially those who are stuck in their own ways. In most cases people like that are only interested in pushing their own agenda. It becomes like the mumbled speech of Charlie Brown's elders, so you tend to block it out. Usually I get to the point of falling asleep when they talk, especially when I know where the conversation is going. When that happens, I take it as a sign that my energy doesn't match up with my environment and I need to move on as quickly as possible.

No matter the circumstances, being taken advantage of is never a good thing, so I always make sure to pay attention. I believe this is another form of protection that the universe has given me. It seems to strengthen and sharpen my awareness. The universe is always in motion and will protect those with good energy. I often think of all the tragic situations that probably occur when I'm not around and it makes me glad that the universe pulled me in another direction. Now that I've finally started listening to the universe and followed the path it put me on, my shield has been repaired and strengthened in a sense. No longer can it be likened to a delicate wood, instead, it is now more of a titanium nature. Of course, I speak metaphorically about changes in life that are inevitable. Things will always change over the course of time and resisting that will only result in you being left behind.

Chapter 13: Told you so

"Underestimating someone is the quickest way to embarrass yourself"

D. Williams

Nothing feels better than looking someone directly in their face and saying the best words in the English language; I told you so.
No matter how many times you are told that something can't be done, or someone belittles you for being different, keep pushing forward and make it happen. There no such thing as "try", just make it happen. Initially this was my reason for getting into business, I just wanted to prove the doubters wrong no matter what the cost. I wanted to break away from certain stereotypes that were cast on me. I never liked labels, so it would piss me off me when people tried to put me in, what they considered an acceptable category.

Unfortunately, my facial expression would always give me away, even if I didn't say anything. The fact is, sometimes people can't help doubting you because of their own brokenness. No matter how genuine you are, they will still find ways to question your sincerity. I have personally been underestimated, counted out and anything else you can think of. At first, I would get so upset that I would cry because I couldn't understand how they came to this conclusion. Now, their assumption has become fuel for my personal motivation. It mostly happens because of my calm demeanor, and that no longer bothers me because that's just my personality. I've gotten to a place where hardly anything gets to me because I'm not defined by people and their warped ideas. I define myself and it was so liberating to come to this realization on my own.
I have mentally told people; "I told you so" because I remember everything. I make mental notes of the things people say, both good and bad. I've always tried to make it clear to people "don't disrespect me in the beginning and then congratulate me later". When this happens, it adds a lot of fuel to my fire. I became relentless in wanting to prove the naysayers wrong. This earned me the reputation of "terminator" because I wouldn't stop for anyone.

Now that I have been able to "shut them up" my priorities have shifted. I'm no longer concerned with simply proving my worth to other people. I'm more worried about the legacy that I want to leave behind. No matter how nice I try to be, I am not going to be liked by everyone. I'm fine with this because I realize some of us don't mesh well with others.

I have shifted from having something to prove to making my "why" have a much deeper reason. Eventually, trying to prove yourself gets old and this urge no longer exists within me. This is a habit I pushed myself to break free of. I feel so much better when I do things simply because I love doing them. I have always said that working for the expectations of others is the quickest way to have yourself working forever.

When I started my journey, I was headstrong because it seemed to be necessary. I felt that I couldn't just let people come along and disrespect me, so in the beginning I always reacted defensively because everything got under my skin. I didn't realize it, but I was pushing away the very people I was asking for help, simply because I couldn't take a joke or unfamiliar comment. If someone didn't buy a product, I would get upset or if something came up on their end, I didn't want to talk to them ever again. I took things personal and felt lied to, even if that wasn't the case. I was new to the world of entrepreneurship and didn't handle rejection very well. These days if I hear "no" I turn my focus back to my goal and keep pushing toward it, unhindered.

Early on it was so paralyzing because I could handle getting rejected once or twice, but my skin wasn't thick enough to handle very many at a time. I now take most of it with a grain of salt and not let it get to me as much as it once did. In the beginning I was told that I was too emotional to be in business, but the truth is; I was passionate, so I pursued business anyway.

Because I love what I do, I didn't want to hear anything that went against it or made me feel I had to change this newfound passion. While I disagree with being ruthless, I do agree that you need to be stern in your footing when it comes to your path. The beautiful thing about this new age we live in, is that there are so many opportunities available that you can easily do 20 things.

When it comes to my accomplishments, I usually don't say out loud to people "I told you so", I allow my actions to do the talking instead. I love when I tell someone my plans or goals and they show doubt and disbelief in me because it revs me up to show and prove. Then as my results start to pour in, they can't get mad since I gave fair warning. I never felt the need to doubt someone else since I have no idea what they're capable of. In fact, I think it's a waste of time to immediately disregard what people say just because you didn't witness it first-hand.

Our society has this "show me, then I'll believe" mentality and I've never agreed with that. If someone asks for proof of something for a valid reason, I support that, but asking for proof just for the sake of being nosey is unacceptable in my opinion. When that happens, I simply say; "don't worry about it". That usually burns people up because they now feel desperate to know what you're doing. Just remember, not everyone should be privy to everything you're doing. If I decide to give someone information, it will be the bare minimum unless it's someone I trust.

I get very irritated when people ask just for the sake of being nosey because I can clearly see their agenda. Sometimes, when you give too much information you get a "yeah, okay" response. When that happens, sometimes you just have to say; "I tried to tell you". Instead of going back and forth with people like that, I find it's better to just prove them wrong.

Silence is a golden response for nosey people. There are advantages to staying silent even though it may seem quite the contrary. Silence allows you to be observant, and that helps prevent others from taking advantage of you. If people know you're unpredictable, your success will take them by surprise. There's been several times when I was able to say; "I told you so" in my mind to people after they immediately showed disbelief when I told them what I planned to accomplish.

Chapter 14: Queens
"Respect the queens; true masters of their kingdoms"

As a male entrepreneur, I can testify to the fact that with the right people on your team, you can take on anything. It took a while, but I have grown out of the mindset of doing everything by myself. It makes things so much easier to talk to people, regardless of where they are in the world.

I have met some great power couples in the world of entrepreneurship in a variety of fields and although most of the people I've met have been female, I have not had any issues. I have a great deal of respect for them and I'm sure they respect me just the same. Having mostly female entrepreneurs in my circle wasn't what I asked for, it just happened that way. Sometimes our conversations are borderline flirtatious, but we keep it professional most of the time.

I also tend to be sarcastic when I speak, but some friends are cool with it. Although some don't care for it, that's honestly part of my character.

I always say that most women I know would put some of us men to shame because of how ridiculously hard they work, and I have a great deal of respect for that.

I consider myself a hard worker by nature, but I must tip my hat to single mothers around the world. There is no one I know that works harder than a woman who is motivated by her children to do something great. I love how some women seem to command respect in the way they carry themselves. They don't have to say anything, it just oozes out of them.

If you are a woman with this type of confidence, don't be afraid to show it. A lot of men wouldn't be here if it wasn't for women like you. This is the reason it bothers me as a man to see a woman mentally, physically and emotionally abused. I was raised by an

Incredibly strong woman, so this always strikes a chord in me when I see it happening to other women, especially one that I am personally affiliated with.

Over the years I've met some great women and I have found that if you have the right woman by your side, she will propel you toward many new things. The right queen will have you question every bad relationship you ever had prior to meeting her. Her blissful energy will have you wanting to build a kingdom with her as your partner. You don't need a lot of women just to make you feel complete. It only takes one queen to capture your heart. That was a lesson I learned early on, so I am always grateful for it.

The beautiful thing about meeting a true queen is that she may physically want you, but she doesn't need or depend on you. I prefer having a strong woman in my corner because they always keep me on my toes. They are always honest with you and expect nothing less in return.

I have always respected single mothers most of all because they work twice as hard as the average person. I am constantly in awe seeing how hard they work despite being a hard worker myself. For me, seeing them is more motivation than competition. In fact, it always makes me step my game up twice as much. Strong women always seem to humble me, probably because my mom is one herself. I didn't realize how much of a role a woman can
play in a man's life until I started meeting them in my own life. There are many quotes that talk about kings and queens and how a man can move mountains with the right woman by his side. A true queen is someone that will stand by your side in war, yet she can tame your animalistic side and keep you from doing things that are irrational. There are not many people that I'll take advice from unless we are in sync with one another.

For the most part, the ladies that are currently in my life have not disappointed me. Maybe it's because I was raised by such a strong woman, so my defenses are not as high around them. I tend to be more resistant with men around, probably as a result of pride; who knows. Throughout my life I have been in the presence of great women who exemplify the role of a true queen. With some of them I have built a great rapport, which is invaluable in the business world. They are proof positive that sometimes a great woman is all you need. Sometimes, I feel that I have met the perfect woman, other times I think she may only exist in a different dimension. Everyone's plan for meeting the right one is different, and I have learned to not rush the process.

Whenever I focus on myself and my work that's when a partner always seems to manifest, but when I'm actively looking, I can't find one at all. So, I made a vow to myself that I would become the best version of me, that way our bond and foundation would be a solid one. I have been broken in the past and it is utterly impossible to fix someone if you yourself are broken. As they say, that's like the blind leading the blind. I have had relationships in the past that didn't work out just like everyone else. I sometimes think they didn't work out because of different levels of complacency. I have always thought on a large scale, so my plans are just as large. This could be an issue if the other person is not 100% on the same page with you. My own eagerness used to get in the way sometimes because I would see my friends settling down in their early 30s and that made me rush to follow their lead because I didn't want to feel left out. I am learning on my journey that the same way I am clear about my business and financial goals, should be the same way I be about my love life. I should be clear and precise about how I want my ideal partner to be. At one point I wasn't doing this because I just wanted love and that's not always enough.

The older I get the clearer I am about how I want my perfect queen to be. Sometimes I get so wrapped up in my business that my love life suffers in return. I've come to realize that the right one is not just going to fall in my lap, I must make time and room for her to be in my life. This is an area of my life that I'm currently working on.

One of my biggest obstacles is that whenever a relationship doesn't work out, I bury myself in my business and block out everything else out. It helps take my mind off the heartbreak and helps me not dwell on it, which is a bad habit of mine.

Experiences like that confirm to me that I have a lot of work to do on myself and that is not a bad thing. Self-development is a necessary part of life and a gateway to our future.

I've met some great women whose journeys have intertwined with my own and now we have each other's back. Even if they become Queens of far-away kingdoms, I will still be there for them whenever they need me. This extension of help is available to those who have put in time with me. My word is always bond and those that know me on a deep level know that if you can get past my stubborn ways, then my loyalty and devotion are both yours. I am not easily accessible to everyone because people will take advantage if you are too open. Thankfully, my circle has not changed drastically.

When it comes to people on your journey, obviously there are sacrifices because everyone can't come with you. However, there are certain people that can't be replaced. Most of my circle has been women, but I didn't even realize this until I was older. I have had male friends, but preferred female friends growing up. I think because I loved deep conversations and it would feel strange to have those conversations with another man. Don't get me wrong, I got along with both well, I just find that I relate more to women. I have also found that some are less judgmental than others, which is what I have always been drawn to. I have always accepted people as they are because I hate to be judged myself, so I make it a point to not do it to others. I often look at friends who have found their other half, and even though I am happy for them finding their queens, it does leave me wondering when I will find my own. Until then, I focus on building my empire, but the thought of it still comes up for me sometimes. This is a powerful lesson in patience that keeps me focused on my journey. Now that I am certain of who I am and how my heart is, I won't just settle for anyone. Our connection must be on a deeper level. The right woman will make you step up whether you want to or not.

She will encourage you because she sees your potential, not just because she wants you to do all the work. Some of my greatest results have happened because of the push I got from the great women around me. They have also become the backbone of my business so I will always value their opinion.

A true King makes all final decisions, but not before consulting with those closest to him.

They say; "this is a man's world", but as the famous James Brown song tells us; "it wouldn't be nothing without a woman or a girl"
When it comes to these great women in my life, their opinions are not meant to be bossy or manipulative, they just give me a new perspective to consider; a piece of wisdom. Since I was raised by such a strong woman, I value them with high esteem. Because of that, I find it easier to be vulnerable around them.

Talking to them has had a profound Impact on my life. I think it's an awesome thing when I see some of them make as much money as men do. I feel it should always be that way. If it wasn't for them, most men would be clueless. They always reassure me that the right one will come along when I'm not looking and that she will find me at the most unexpected time and place.

As a naturally ambitious person, I'm always on the move, so this is the part of my life where I'm learning to be still. I'm grateful for the
women in my circle because they are always teaching me about how different women think. We don't see eye to eye all the time, but it never gets disrespectful and we can always have a civilized conversation about where we disagree. Most of them are older so they always tell me that they don't have time for bullshit and petty arguments. Being a traditional man, I can respect that.

Believe it or not, it was a woman that pushed me to want to be a billionaire in the first place. Not just someone in my circle, but someone by the name of Sarah Blakely, who founded the company Spanx. There are many examples of female billionaires and I think the number is starting to catch up to men. I'm not threatened by it actually and deeply respect it. I think women are just as capable as men when it comes to success.

Whether you want to be the next billionaire or have set the bar lower or aren't an entrepreneur at all. I personally don't have a problem with women making as much as men. From a team perspective, it should be encouraged. If both people are on the same page, you can truly move mountains when it comes to your goals and aspirations. Not only have I moved mountains with the females around me, I have masterminded some of my best ideas with them. The same can also be said with some of my past relationships.

Chapter 15: Gladiator School

"Business is like fighting, you never know who wants to take your position"

If you notice me use the term "gladiator school" I'm not talking about a physical arena. I'm taking about the experiences we go through and how tough they are like fighting in a training simulator. When it comes to fighting, life is very much the same way, especially in the business arena. When you first start, you pick your fighting technique, but your moves are terrible, and you stumble over yourself. Your punches don't pack much power and your awareness needs a lot of work. That's okay because this is just the beginning stage and although it feels like an eternity, things will get better.

You begin to enhance your fighting technique and each day you notice a little more progress. Mastering business is just like mastering a style of fighting, but most people may not notice the similarities.

I have always been fascinated with kickboxing in particular because of the techniques it employs, so I use that as my business mindset. I didn't always look at business this way, but I now see how the mentality is just alike.

Some people enter the arena, then quit before they see results. The lifestyle looks glamorous on the outside, but in reality; it's not very pretty and a lot of hard work. People only see the results, but you must go through the full process to experience it for yourself.

In this microwave society we live in, everyone wants the quick and easy version. The fact is that some things in life can't be rushed. Sometimes I feel like a fish out of water because I was raised with different standards than the kids of today. Whether you are building a multi-billion-dollar company or pursuing the highest level of education, the grind is the same.

It comes with long nights, paperwork everywhere, eating fast food, and watching motivational videos to keep you going. There are parts of the process I dislike, and most people will probably feel the same, but it always pays off in the end. I have learned from my gladiator school experience to protect my space and not allow people to damage my armor. In the past I have indeed taken some hard hits to both the body and face, but I keep pushing forward.

I'm the type of person who never gives up and doesn't take no for an answer. Once my mind is made up on something, it's hard to change it.

The legendary martial artist Bruce Lee said it best; "I fear not the man who has practiced 10,000 kicks once, but I fear the man who has practiced one kick 10,000 times." In other words, perfect your craft.

In the business world, a common, ongoing debate is whether one should focus and master one thing or have more of a diverse portfolio. I think it depends on the area of expertise you choose, but I have found it easier to focus on one area at a time, then move on to something else.

When it comes to gladiator school, it's always a learning experience, which is not a bad thing. In fact, it's a blessing because it helps you master the area of expertise you have chosen.

As a child, I watched my fair share of fighting shows, such as UFC, WWE and Dragon Ball Z. I was always fascinated by how different fighting styles matched up with their opponents.

There's something about reaching a state of calmness during a fight, when your confidence is high, and you know that the opposition can't predict your next move. That same state of mind applies in business just the same. I like to call it your Zen place. It's like reaching the peak of mental awareness.

This is a key lesson I learned from watching Dragon Ball Z. Whenever there's a battle, those who fight with rage always lose to those who have reached their Zen place. When it comes to this fighting mentality, Bruce Lee is quoted as saying;

*"The highest technique is no technique
My technique is a result of your technique.
My movement is a result of your movement"*

I'm currently striving to reach my "Zen place" in life and in business. A place where I can rule the moment and allow nothing to shift my focus. I spend a lot of time in solitude for this exact reason, and because I am reading the right books that feed my mind, I am closer to reaching my Zen place than ever.

Sometimes I feel like I've lived this life before because people always say I have an old soul. I tend to view things differently from the average person and people naturally trust me more than others. I think others sense a certain energy or sincerity in me, so they warm up to me even faster than I warm up to them.
I also feel the presence of my grandfather exuding from me.
Only after seeing the example he set, I started to take life more seriously. Before that I lived carefree and never worried about any responsibilities. Although, as you grow older and start to see people around you pass on, it has a way of bringing you back to reality.

I want necessarily a problem child. I didn't have anger issues or anything like that. I simply preferred doing what I thought was right at the moment instead what I was told by my elders. Once when I was a kid, I took one of my mom's checks, went to a restaurant by myself and wrote it for $1,000. Of course, I didn't know what the hell I was doing, so I handed the server this extra-large check, thinking everything was cool. Instead, she proceeded to call the police and I was escorted to school.

Thank the heavens they couldn't arrest me because of my age, but I learned a lot from that experience. That was my first lesson in business because I felt like a boss that day. Even though the situation didn't escalate too high that day, it felt incredible to have that check in my hand. I didn't know it at the time, but that turned out to be a glimpse into my future dealings. I have often been told that what you do as a child is symbolic of who you will be as an adult and I have found that to be true.

As someone who has studied fighting styles, I want my business moves to be based on the same mental instincts. I want them to be executed so effortlessly that it becomes second nature.

Another lesson I learned from watching Dragon Ball Z is from two fighters; Goku and Vegeta, whose personalities are completely different. Goku is very silly yet fighting comes natural to him. Vegeta, on the other hand, is much more serious and is often encouraged to loosen up. He is also an exceptional fighter in his own right.

The greatest thing I have learned from all of this is mastery. It's not about beating your opponent with 1,000 different moves. It only takes one move, if mastered, to defeat anyone. It starts with self-mastery. Once you master yourself, you have already defeated your opponent. You'll be able to anticipate their every move quickly and effortlessly. In any battle, make your fight brief and to the point. It shouldn't be about being flashy with fancy moves. It should be about ending the fight as soon as possible. It never occurred to me that business would ever correlate with fighting. Sometimes, the best lessons are learned just by studying fighting techniques. Using brute strength and punching your way through something is never the smart way to go. You must use strategy, as in a game of chess. Each move must be calculated and well thought out. The best fighters in the world approach any battle in this manner. They have already defeated you in the mind before the battle even takes place.

Years ago, I was much more aggressive and not much of a thinker. In fact, I have done some very foolish things. Thankfully, social media wasn't around back then, or I would have a lot of explaining to do.

After having a conversation with a friend, I can see that my high respect for women comes from being raised by one. My mother was a solid figure in my life when it came to standards, which is why I have such high respect for women. Those standards and principles have influenced my dealings with other women in my life as well. That is why I often say that I respect strong women because I was raised by one. And no matter how upset a situation makes me, you will never hear me call women "bitch" because it would be weird to say. Out of every cuss word I've ever used, that one would be the least. It just doesn't sit well with me.

Chapter 16: Don't skip on freedom

I haven't always been so determined or ambitious. In fact, at one time, I stayed far away from responsibility. In my younger years, I frequently skipped class, especially in Highschool. I mostly did this with classes like math and social studies. It was never a question of intellect; it was more about application. Any time I fully applied myself, my grades were very high. During this phase, I felt that I didn't fit in with my classmates. I felt like I was trapped at school, so I started looking for a way out. After getting a taste of freedom away from school, I became addicted and would do anything in my power to get more of it. I would like just to get out of class. Sometimes, I would go to school for half the day then find a reason to go home early. I did it so frequently, they started to monitor me in a daily basis. They would call my mom just to make sure I went to school. As a person who loves their Independence, this stuck a nerve. I hated knowing that someone was always watching and micromanaging my every move. This ended up being my introduction to freedom and Independence because I hated living life under someone else's thumb. Because of this, writing became my new outlet. Being able to express myself with such freedom was so liberating.

I absolutely love the movie Freedom writers. It's based on the best-selling book the Freedom Writers diary by Erin Gruwell. During that time, I was just getting into fully expressing myself. Prior to transitioning into my business path, I had no idea what freedom of expression truly was. I felt trapped, almost suffocated in the shadow of a 9 to 5, micromanaged, lifestyle. This, is why, at my age I have so many ideas bubbling up within me. I was suppressed for such a long time and now that I have free range to do what I want; ideas pretty much just spill out of my brain. It's at a point where the ideas are getting hard to control, so I'm careful about who I share them with.
I believe entrepreneurship has always been in me, just lying dormant. When it comes to life, people around me could always tell that I wanted more than just being average. Even though my drive is mostly internal, I sometimes get the external push when I watch something motivational on YouTube or a good movie.

Eric Thomas is one of my personal favorites because of his passion when he speaks. He worked his way up from the bottom and earned his spot. There's something about a rags-to-riches story that automatically gets my attention. It might be because I prefer to work my way up rather than find shortcuts. The fact is, there is no fast track to success, you must take the stairs.

It's so easy to want to take the escalator on your path to success, but eventually that would get boring. Taking the stairs lets you admire the scenery and cherish the memories, but most of all, it gives you a sense of accomplishment, knowing you earned your spot at the top.
Getting a taste of freedom is like a slice of your favorite cheesecake. Once you take a bite you'll keep coming back for more.
When your mentality is timid it's hard to say no, even to the most unreasonable requests, but living on your own terms makes you strong enough to say no without hesitation if you so choose.
Ironically enough, I am now a freedom writer and I encourage others to express themselves freely as well. I am very proud to be a contributor to that movement in my own way because their message is synonymous with one of the messages I like to spread.

Sometimes I feel like an unofficial spokesperson for entrepreneurship because I love it just that much. Don't get me wrong, I don't tell people what to do or how to do it when it comes to entrepreneurship, but I do nudge them in that direction if they express frustration with their current situation. I have really started to view my ventures as forms of expression and not just business. That's why I'm all in at this point. It lets me express myself the way that I choose and not conform to everyone else's ways. There's no turning back for me and I am in this journey until it's over.

Chapter 17: Worthy

For as long as I can remember, I felt unworthy when it came to the title of King. Growing up, I was always called by mean names, even when I was minding my own business. It was the one of the worst feelings I ever experienced and back then It hurt me to the core. At one point I didn't think I would ever get away from that. I thought they were just out to get me. I used to drive myself crazy trying to figure out what I did to deserve it.
These days my life has been so fulfilling since then, so I no longer think about it. Believe it or not, surviving that helped me develop a strong work ethic. The biggest lesson I took away from the experience was that self-worth comes from within. You must feel worthy inside before others can see you that way.

When I was younger, I spent a lot of time looking for outside validation. I used to be scared to even ask questions and would break out in a sweat when someone tried talking to me. I was socially awkward and avoided people at all costs. I was easily intimidated and preferred not to be in front of large groups of people. Public speaking, especially in large venues was also difficult for me. Public speaking in large venues was just not my thing. I don't think it was an issue of low self-esteem. I think that I was just psyching myself out. Often, we are the stumbling blocks that get in our own way.

Around this time, I started reading about people who overcame adversity in their own lives and accomplished great things despite their disabilities. A prime example of this is Daymond John, who in 1992 founded a company called FUBU. Daymond was diagnosed with dyslexia, yet he did not allow this to prevent him from making his dreams come true. Today, the hip hop apparel company has a net worth of $300 million. Daymond is also one of several multi-millionaires on the show Shark Tank where wealthy entrepreneurs invest their own money in the ideas and products of upcoming entrepreneurs. I used people like Daymond as inspiration to build my own dreams and I even gave thought to perhaps creating my own apparel brand in the future. I'm sure that there's competition in every industry, but I tend to stay in my lane and do my own thing. If I allowed myself to focus on how much competition there was out there, I would never have entered the arenas that I'm currently in. I would have probably been too intimidated to even try.

For a long time, I rejected leadership and anyone that challenged me to step up. I avoided it because deep down I felt unworthy, although there were some people around me that saw my potential and tried to encourage me. Unfortunately, I was told for so long that what I wanted "couldn't be done" so I focused on that instead. Now that I have freed myself from the chains of low self-esteem, I will die before I let anyone have that much power over me again. When I reflect on my chosen path and the importance of freedom, there's a quote that comes to mind;

"The price of freedom is high, and it is a price I'm willing to pay." - Captain America: The Winter Soldier (Evans 2014).

That quote gives me peace of mind and I have truly embraced it. I am always mindful of how long it took me to get to a place of such confidence. This is the reason I'm so selective of those I let into my space. I only invite those who build me up, not tear me down. Low self-esteem was something I battled with daily and knowing that these types of challenges would continue to present themselves I had to make a change. Now that my self-esteem is high, I feel worthy of everything that happens. I've been able to handle any changes and developments with my business because I'm determined not to let the opinions of others hinder what I do.

I've been able to flow with all the changes and developments of my businesses and I am determined not let the opinions of others hinder what I do. Learning the skills to overcome my weaknesses was an endless battle at times.
You may never know what to expect, but that is what makes it exciting. When you start to make changes in your life be ready for anything and do not let your fears get in the way. Know your worth and stand by it. Shine your light; others will see it and be drawn to it as well. That doubtful voice in the back of your mind may always taunt you, but never let it win. It's important for you not to let that inside voice talk you out of doing something that might change your life. There were days where I knew what to do, and sometimes I still second guessed myself. I'm glad that in most cases, I trusted the direction my intuition was leading me. Following your intuition helps you block out that voice inside your head that makes you question everything. One way that I overcame this voice was reducing the amount of television I watched. All the negativity constantly shown from the media had a massive effect on me, so it warped my thinking.

I always try to be appreciative of what I have, so I try to keep my mind focused on gratitude. Watching the news, full of negative occurrences in society that I had no control over would disrupt my thinking, my flow, and overall spirit, so I avoid it. I want nothing more than to stay focused on my path and steadfast in this new feeling of worthiness in my heart and mind. I found myself almost obsessed with YouTube and the wide array of motivational videos available on the Internet. My confidence was strengthened through watching countless videos and I am confident that if a motivational form of media was not available for me throughout my adult life, then I would not be where I am today. I remember a time when suicide seemed like a viable option. I was often unsure of what I would do or who I would become. For the longest time there was a sense of never feeling good enough or matching up to my peers. How would I ever be worthy enough to even dream of being on a platform with the likes of incredible, successful entrepreneurs like Eric Thomas?

Although debilitating, my condition of unworthiness was self-inflicted, so I always remind myself of all the work that I put in to get where I am today. It was no easy feat getting to this point of confidence, so I refuse to go back to the days of feeling unworthy.

Since that time, I have broken free of the mental prison I was trapped in for so long. Sadly enough, when you are unable to see past the walls around you, it stops you from seeing any progress outside of that.

Now that I have a taste of freedom, I will never allow anyone to put my mind in captivity again. In the past, whenever someone tried to convince me that I didn't have a shot at my dreams I always found it helpful to change the subject to something positive. I learned different techniques that enabled me to become my own "security guard". I was in control of who came in, who got close, and who offered the most beneficial support to my brands.

I learned to read people and sense when their energy did not match the direction I was going. I made mental notes of the things people would say to me, either directly or indirectly. I began to react differently when I felt someone was too doubtful of my actions. If they were not adding value to my current situation, then they simply were not worthy to be part of it.

I always encourage others to be cognizant of their worth. Wear it like a badge of honor and be proud of who you are always. No other person should have enough of a hold on you to dictate who you are. In my opinion, anyone who does this can go fuck themselves. Pardon my language, but if they don't know you from a whole in the wall, they should have no say-so over your life. Being guided is something I'm always open to but being controlled is a different story. The minute I feel this way, I immediately find something else to do that will get me away from the source of this anguish. I wasn't always able to pick up on this, but after being in situations like that countless times, eventually you wake up and start to pay attention to how people operate. Having someone take advantage of your kindness becomes a cautionary event, so it causes your thinking to shift when dealing with others. This is the sort of thing that would happen to me before I became a man of strong principles and found my worth. I remember when I was considered a "yes" man at one time. It pissed me off because people would only judge me by what they saw on the outside instead of trying to get the full story. You can explain things to people all day long, but if their mind is already made up, you're just wasting your time.

Chapter 18: Moments of Surrealism

I am currently at a point of enjoying and loving life. These days I have been presented with awesome opportunities that I once asked for, but never thinking whether they would manifest themselves or not. I have a habit of asking for things and never thinking twice about them afterward. That's probably why opportunities always seem to find me because I don't overthink then. You attract what you think of most, so if you overthink things, which is a form of doubt, the universe responds alike. If you believe in a higher power, then doubt should never be in your heart. I believe, so I'm all in.

I finally decided to jump off the cliff and begin soaring. No longer worried about when I will gain momentum or if I feel the air under my wings. By the age of 30, I finally made up for
all the time I spent being lazy or undecided about life. Being in talks with companies such as Target, Walgreens, QVC and Sephora about my fragrance line, feels like I'm floating. I sometimes must take a step back and realize that I have done a lot and now my efforts are paying off. I am genuinely passionate about all that I do, so to me, it doesn't feel like work. I am just a guy from Queens working his way up the mountain; at least that is how I looked at it for a long time. I am just now learning that it is okay to take a break. Taking a break does not mean the job is finished, it just means you're recharging. I am now learning that I do not have to be a workaholic all the time. At this point, I believe I have earned a break or two.

There have been some moments in my life that I can only describe as surreal. Being on cruises in the Bahamas, sitting in a Lamborghini, seeing the inside of penthouses and even mansions to say the least. I guess I have
expensive taste because I've always been into that stuff like that. I have made other business moves such as speaking to companies like Black Enterprise and Entrepreneur magazine in order to expand my brands.

There were other business opportunities that I reached out to but never heard anything back from. This honestly does not bother me because I can at least say that I did it. I thank God, the universe and/or the powers that be for giving me this vision at a relatively early age. I was a late bloomer in thinking big, but I have found my own way to catch up to everyone else. Although risky, I have always preferred to take my chances on certain things. I no longer believe in playing it safe because your results will always be average.

Now that my own life is starting to take off, and I am staying busy with many things and I choose opportunities more wisely. Life is awesome and most of all surreal if you allow it to be. The only thing you need to do is make a decision and not let other people make you feel guilty about it. I was once guilty of sometimes getting in my own way because I would overthink and dwell on things that I shouldn't. It's most definitely a difficult habit to break. To combat this, I leave my electronics at home and just go for a walk. This has been the most helpful because it leaves me alone with my thoughts and helps me escape the overwhelming digital world. I used to be addicted to technology, but I am glad I was able to break away from it. I did not realize how much time I wasted until I took a step back. One of my mentors recently had me do an experiment where I recorded everything I did throughout the day, hour by hour.
At first it was strange because I had never done it before, but afterwards it made me so much more productive. It has helped me to manage my time better and rid myself of the things that waste my time. Initially, I hated it and couldn't understand the concept, but I have learned that a lot of the world's most successful people do this. I wanted a better life, and this was a step in that direction. I realized I was just coasting around when it came to how I devoted my time, so nothing was being properly delegated.

Another one if my mentors said "if you want to be a billionaire, then act like one and own your
time". Even though this hurt at the time, it was something I needed to hear. I wasn't managing my time very well, yet I kept claiming that I wanted to be a multi-millionaire and billionaire.

Even though my mentor and I don't communicate daily, because of my chosen path, I deeply value his advice. His words keep me mindful of having a blueprint drawn out so that I'm not just coasting along letting the wind push me in random directions.

Over the course of several months, I began implementing a structured business plan, and as a result, my entrepreneur life started to flow seamlessly. The foundation for it began to solidify and my goals were starting to be met. I often wonder what level my goals would be at today, if only I came across the proper mentors and friends earlier on my journey.
I have learned a tremendous amount on this journey, and I am forever grateful for that. Even though I wish I started earlier, I'm grateful for what I have because gratitude is always better than regret. It's the difference between forward and backward thinking.

Another joyful and surreal moment in my life was being able to visit the Forbes building. This may seem small to some, but it was monumental for me because I have read and admired their magazine for quite some time. I also follow and admire entrepreneur magazine. I took a chance on contacting them because I realized that behind every huge corporation there are still regular people just like us.

I must admit, large corporations used to intimidate me because I would always assume that their employees would be assholes and just blatantly rude. However, after several phone conversations with their representatives, they
have been some of the nicest people I have spoken to. These small moments on my path to success were the universe's way of letting me know that my dreams were attainable. It also let me know I was in the best energy flow and doing things at the right time.

When approaching these companies, I had a David versus goliath mindset. I always felt small because my finances weren't at the level that I wanted them to be when I took these bold steps. I always thought "what if they want to move forward and I'm not ready?" Eventually, I remembered what I did when I put my first book out. I stopped over analyzing and just went for it and it ended up paying off. They gave me all the information I needed to work with them.

Because I have a colossal mind and always think on a large scale, I tend to overcomplicate things. It happened one time when I was an intern for a non-profit organization called the New York State Youth Leadership Council. The name alone made me think it was going to be a fancy place with a corporate appearance, conference room and everything. Although, it wasn't quite as fancy as I thought It would be, I learned a lot about respecting people internationally. My main point is, don't get attracted to how something sounds; do your research. The name of that company had me excited, but once I got there my ego was quickly deflated.

I've always been addicted to shiny things and titles that sound important, so the names of each company I contacted had me excited the moment I heard them. Once I got past all of that, it was easy to contact them. Some of them didn't respond, but at least I can say that I did it.
Eventually, my mentality shifted, so rejection never bothered me again. I can always say at least I tried and have no regrets. So, I made a conscious decision that every opportunity that comes to me, if it's fun and compatible with my journey, I'm taking it. Sometimes even random opportunities to travel came to me and I took them without hesitation. Sometimes you must be a little impulsive and I refuse to be a "shoulda, coulda, woulda" person.

Chapter 19: Operation Yellow Brick Road

I have a program that I'm working on called "Operation Yellow Brick Road". It started from a conversation I had with a dear friend about my current level of accomplishment as an entrepreneur.
Operation Yellow Brick Road is going to be a mentoring program for those that live with disabilities. After doing volunteer work with them, I noticed that there were not a lot of programs that help them with getting employment, so I want to be that resource for them. I want to eventually set up partnerships
with grooming businesses like barbershops and places that make suits. I have a definite plan for each of my ventures, and they will all intertwine with one other. At first, I didn't see it this way. When I think about all the different jobs I worked in the past, compared to now, the different businesses that I have and those to come, I never saw this coming.

I love that my work ethic is so strong to the point that it inspires people. I have recently started to look at it like a yellow brick road that I am paving for others to follow. It honestly went from a light conversation to speaking about a serious non-profit business proposal rather quickly. I had other ideas, but I felt this one went perfect with the projects I am already doing. Yellow brick road would be an amazing "icing on the cake" when It comes to my accomplishments. At first it didn't feel like a big deal, but when I think of other people my age, this is huge.

I always feel as though I was spiritually pushed on to this path. I love that I have found people who don't suppress my ideas, but instead encourage them. When I was younger, I felt trapped in the small box that society has drawn for us. I was always anxious for the opportunity to break free, so each of my achievements are a long time coming.

This is also the reason I keep my choices to myself. The more people know about your plans, the more they feel obligated to talk you out of them. It makes me feel intruded upon, especially since my mind is already made up.

The idea of becoming a billionaire was exciting for me, there again I looked at it like a yellow brick road that I could build as wide, straight, or narrow as I choose. The best part, no one controls this road except me. I started to approach all my decisions and projects in the "yellow brick road" concept. It's simple; I leave a blueprint and legacy for the world by being myself, being resilient and letting my voice be heard. At some point I realized I am no longer satisfied with simply "getting by" and being a follower. I looked for an outside savior and when no one came, I had to get my ass up and get shit done.

The idea of just doing what I was told always felt like I was in grade school, needing permission for small things like going to the bathroom. I despise the idea of being "micromanaged" and knowing that people don't trust me to make my own judgement. Despite what others may think, my name will be synonymous with many brands. From perfume to wine, to fashion, and one day, even a hotel. The beautiful part is, they will all work together. Some of my business ventures are future ideas, but I strongly feel that whatever you devote your time to will manifest.

I have big plans for everything in my life. Just imagine how amazing it would be to have my hotel business as the central headquarters for my other businesses. The idea of a hotel having a perfume store, champagne store and fashion store in one place sounds awesome to me. I'm glad that I met people along the way that always help me manifest all these ideas step by step on my journey as an entrepreneur. It makes me laugh when people ask me if I ever sleep after working on so many amazing ideas. I usually joke with them and say; "no I don't sleep". It looks very hectic, but I have learned to spread my days out, so that it doesn't drive me crazy. I have been told that I make all my work look easy, but that's how I do it, just spread things out.

My other strategy is simply writing things down. It's a classic method that will never disappoint. It allows you to stay focused on what's important in the moment and reserve other ideas for their perfect time.

Operation yellow brick road is near and dear to me because it gives me a new perspective on life and how important it is to give back. It is amazing what a simple conversation can spark and how far it can go if you just have faith. I honestly don't take credit for my ideas; I give that to God. I'm just a messenger who will go to the ends of the earth to get things done. The concept for this future non-profit came from observing people with special needs and seeing that there were not a lot of programs that groom them for employment.

Of all my accomplishment, I feel that this would be the icing on the cake for my life. I've always loved helping others by giving back and I'm happy to be a light in someone else's dark tunnel. When I started this journey, I didn't have a lot of help, so I had to be my own cheerleader for a long time. Because of that, I had a bit of a chip on my shoulder, so even if someone eventually offered help, I might have rejected it.

Now that I've worked my way up to a higher level, people are paying more attention and even though I was reluctant, I have started to receive and accept the help of others. I have dropped my restraints and have decided to accept whatever help comes my way, if it comes from a genuine place. I always say that it's not what you say, but how you say it, so I pay attention when people communicate with me. You can usually tell in a person's tone and body language whether they mean you well or not.

Having been through a lot while building my brands, it has heightened my awareness of other people's mannerisms. In the past I felt double-crossed by many people, so I developed a sense of paranoia because of the way they acted when I discussed my business ventures.

Despite normally being open to meeting new people and developing relationships, those bad experiences caused me to expect more of the same disappointment or even rejection. I assumed that if I expected it, I could be prepared and not let it take me by surprise. It took a while, but I was finally able to shift my mindset and grow stronger because of that. When I think about it, I laugh because if I could have bet money each time that I had a bad experience, I would be a rich man right now.

As I continue to build my proverbial yellow brick road, it reminds me of something I heard in a man of steel movie;

*"They will race behind you. They will stumble. They will fall,
but in time they will join you in the sun"*.

This always makes me think of those that I have inspired and anyone I may inspire in the future to do bigger and better things. My goal is to challenge people to stop thinking within the realm of their paycheck and think of what's possible. I used to think small as well, but thankfully I met people who did the same thing for me. At this point, in my opinion, it's about paying it forward. I met people who think big and they encouraged me to do the same I feel it's my duty to pass it along to help others think bigger and change their programming. Obviously, I don't force them, but I do plant a seed in their mind if they are open to it. It has been said;

"you can show someone treasure but can't make them think wealthy".

This is the reason that Operation Yellow Brick Road is so important to me. My businesses are brick foundations and I want the road to be strong yet smooth, inlaid with gold. I also want it to be as beautiful and as awe inspiring as possible. My goal is that once people start on this road, they will stay inspired to go all the way to the end. In most cases it's easy to get side-tracked, so I implore you to stay vigilant and determined.

Chapter 20: Slide shows

If you have ever seen a slide show, I'm sure you know that it is meant to tell a story though pictures and most say that this is what life is; one big slide show. My question is; why would you spend your life taking low quality pictures and letting someone be shaky with the camera? Never again will I let someone dictate to me how I should live. If you want a Mercedes or whatever car speaks to you, do not let others convince you to get a Toyota instead. All too often we have our hearts set on something and someone comes out of left field, questioning our choice and that causes us to second guess our decision.

At one point I allowed the uninformed opinions of others to make me question my own decisions. The fact is, I never make my life about things, I make it about experiences, so whatever I choose is based on an experience and that's all that needs to be said.

I have gotten to a point where I am very transparent about what I want in life and it isn't my issue to explain why I want it. If I choose to do so, it is my choice to make. In the past I could always tell when I was taking bad advice and dealing with the wrong person because I start to fumble or make mistakes just to do what they say. I knew in my heart that it wasn't a good fit, but I did it anyway just to be accepted. That's no way for anyone to live.

For the most part I love my slide show. From cruises in the Bahamas, to trips in Canada, I have been to some awesome places. I have never really been a complainer because I feel that I live a blessed life overall. I have taken some wrong turns here and there, but I have always been able to bounce back quickly. My slide show so far has been amazing. I have also traveled to the Cayman Islands and this is only a small part of my slide show. Sitting in a Lamborghini was another dream come true, now the next step is to get one. I can honestly say that I have lived a life most would only dream of. I have no speech issues. I can go wherever I want to go and articulate well enough to communicate with whoever I want.

No matter how expensive my taste is, I never think of myself as "too good" for something. On top of that, my heart always bleeds for the less fortunate that are unable to help themselves. Especially the homeless; I have deep sympathy for them and if I'm ever able to help, I do so. It's second nature for me to assist others and sometimes I get so passionate about it, I must remind myself that I can't save everyone.

Life has ups and downs for everyone, but when something doesn't go right for me, I never really complained, even though I get frustrated like anyone else. I always feel like complaining doesn't fix anything, so I try my hardest to not do it. Even though I've done some things I'm not happy about and things don't always go my way, I like to look at the bigger picture. This is often intimidating when you look at it entirely, but it is easier to take small steps that lead to victories over time.

One of the things I have learned as a billionaire-under-construction, is that there are no shortcuts on the road to success. Sometimes I wish there was an elevator, but at the same time, it would be boring if you could immediately get to your destination. If that was the case, we would never appreciate anything. We are naturally more appreciative when we earn what we have. I have always preferred doing things the old-fashioned way because "easy" was never interesting to me. There is saying that goes;
"anything worth having isn't easy and anything easy isn't worth having".

I have personally found this to be true. Whether in friendships or growing a business, great things take time. I have developed a lot of patience on my journey because at one time I wanted things when I wanted them and wasn't willing to wait. But even waiting isn't always the answer. I was taught that nothing comes from simply waiting. Because of that I have always been against sitting around watching the clock.

I've learned the concept of being aggressively patient, which is the idea of working toward one blessing while waiting for another. If my life were a slideshow, there would be snapshots of vacation visits, cruises, images of exotic cars, bus trips and so on. These are only a few of the snippets of my life. This is part of the reason I don't complain because most of my experiences have been awesome. There have been rough patches for sure, but I have also seen paradise as well. I have seen so many great things that when I encounter sour people, I still make lemonade.

Looking at life like a slide show will make you watch who you allow to hold the camera. I want my pictures and experiences to be as clear as possible, so I'm careful about who gets close to me. Moments of life are very clear when you invite friends who compliment you. I don't mean compliment in a congratulatory sense about your appearance, but someone whose energy intermingles well with yours. People like that, I always ask jokingly; "where have you been all my life?" Those are the ones I'm happy to have in my slide show. These days my slide shows are beautiful to look at. Sure, some pictures aren't perfect, but the good outweigh the bad and I'm happy for that. My slide show will have more laughs then cries. As they say; "laughter is the best medicine".

When I look back over my life, from certificate programs to the places I've travelled to, I want to knock as many things off my list as I can. I know there's going to come a point where I can no longer do certain things because of my age. So, I made a vow to always take my chances.

Chapter 21. Untamed Spirit

"Chase your dreams with a Ferrari engine" D. Williams

Full speed ahead has become one of my favorite things to say. Sometimes people want you to stop and wait for them, which means do things on their terms. The time you spend waiting for people to help or even acknowledge you, can be done by your own self. In my years as an entrepreneur, I have learned to be aggressively patient, which as I previously stated, is the concept of asking for one blessing while working toward another.

Some have told me to slow down, but I have no plans to do so. When it comes to building this dream, I stopped waiting for people a long time ago. It's been said that if you wait for people, you'll be waiting the rest of your life. I've always had the mindset that if people want to help, that's great and if they don't, I'll still get where I'm going. As they say, if one doesn't help, another one will. This doesn't make you impatient. It simply means you are not letting one person slow down your success. Stay clear of those that make you feel that the credit for your success belongs to them. No matter how much a person helps you, it's not sincere if they can't wait to throw it in your face.

As someone whose personality is that of an untamed horse that used to be tamed, it feels better to be on the other side of the fence where you don't have to seek permission or approval for things that you want to do. For a long time, I felt like a horse in a stall. I had so many talents and abilities that I was eager to find out about, yet I was letting others have all the control. The worst part was, I didn't realize it because I was a kind-hearted person. I thought that being soft-spoken while they told me what to do was how I should be. I had so many ideas, yet I was around people who didn't allow me to express them. So, now that I am older and doing my own thing, many ideas spill out of my brain.

I laugh often because I do feel like an untamed horse in my own right. There is something amazing about being untamed in your daily life. My motto has always been *"If everyone else goes to the left, I'm going to the right"*.
I'm just that type of untamed person. And because I don't like to conform to what others do, I don't like large crowds either.

From a business standpoint, I am very untamed. I have a "King of the world" attitude because I spent a lot of time trying to fit into other people's boxes. Now that I can do what I want to do in a sense, I'm taking advantage of it. There is such a strong sense of freedom that comes with an untamed personality. Now that I have a taste of it, I don't want to go back to go being confined.
Being untamed is not just a business mentality, it's something that should be experienced throughout all aspects of life. It is a place that is euphoric in the mind.

Have you ever loved someone with an untamed spirit? It is very different from being with a structured spirit. An untamed spirit is always on the move, searching for something better or just more variety. Even in the realm of sex, an untamed spirit isn't a bad thing, unless you like the same old boring routine.
My mind was blown when I encountered people that wanted to experiment with different positions and places. Before these encounters, I had been restricted to just sex in the bedroom. I am intrigued by those that like making love in different places. On the counter, in the laundromat, on the grass or on the beach. Imagine the waves and sand on the beach hitting you while you are intimate with your partner. There are very few people that have known how deep my mind runs. This is how I know that I'm untamed. I have come to the grips that I love living this way. I have always been an enigma, mysterious to most, but the ones that know me on a deeper and personal level never want to leave. I have not met many who stimulate me intellectually, so, when I am fortunate enough to have the Universe place those types of people in my life, pheromones kick in and these people perhaps catch a rare glimpse of my untamed side. This is my inner core exposed; it often throws people off because I am calm by nature. It is a sight to behold for the few that get to witness when I am out of character like this. I always keep my untamed side in check until I know the other person is worthy.

I have always hated the idea of bowing down to people and the idea that you are expected to just do as you're told, so I made it my personal mission to live an untamed life. This is mainly the reason why I don't limit my conversations with people. I believe that you can't truly know a person unless you have a stimulating conversation with them. This is part of the reason I'm not so caught up in first impressions. Usually the ones you assume won't fit end up being the perfect puzzle piece, and the ones you think are perfect end up being a bad fit. This is part of being untamed because you are no longer obligated if they don't live up to the impression that they gave you the first time. It's really freeing to just get up and go without seeking permission if things don't work out. Your free of being disappointed by other people who don't follow through, free to make as much money as you want to make, and free to think on your own terms.

These are all aspects of being untamed. Being completely free to express yourself without being stifled. I've had a small taste of this level of freedom, so it is a never-ending pursuit to stay this way. The untamed life is the ability to just get up and go without having to check in with people. The ability to country hop or have a villa in the most beautiful spots on the planet and not worrying at all about the price. The ability to walk into a dealership and pay cash for any car you have your eye on.
That is what I call living an untamed life or you could call it the untamed spirit. I always said that I wanted to spin a globe and wherever it stops, that's where I'd go. Not telling anyone except for those that want to go with me. That Is
the epitome of being untamed. I plan to do this with friends that think just like I do. It is always refreshing to encounter friends that have their own passports and travel on their own terms. Being untamed doesn't mean being reckless and sloppy about living life, it just means not being confined.

Chapter 22 Together

"How do you plan to defeat them? Together. What if we lose?
Then we will do that together too" Avengers. Age of Ultron

When I think of teamwork, there are some Iconic duos that come to mind. Iron man and Captain America, Ryu and Ken, Batman and Superman. Black panther and storm. The same applies to business. All you need is one person that comes along and really believes in what you are doing. The beautiful thing about this is that you can find people that compliment you extremely well. I am so glad that I found a person that compliments me. It makes the journey easier because they can do one thing while you do something else. It took a while for me to get used to this because I was used to doing everything myself. These small steps will add up to something bigger in the end.

If you look at everything from a large scale, you might be intimidated. Eventually, you get to a point where doing it all by yourself isn't enough. Everyone needs help to some degree and it's ok to ask. When it comes to building my brands, I have done a lot on my own but I still reached a point where I needed help, so I asked. It is said that you can't become a billionaire on your own. The beautiful thing about this is that you can pick and choose who you want to work with. My friend is very organized, so I joke with her a lot about having a list for everything, but the fact is, her organizing has paid off in my life as well. This is what I was asking from the universe all along.

When it comes to getting things done, I can certainly hold my own, so I just wanted someone to push me to do better. It was difficult at first, for me to deal with someone that wanted to be around me despite our differences, but I think it's the differences that blend is together and not the similarities. She has a way of protecting from the shadows and I on the other hand, like to feel like I do a lot on my own, so our friendship works very well. In metaphorical terms, it's like having a shield next to me, ready to defend me or anyone who stands with me. As a team we have been able to get a lot done. And even though I have had others requesting to work with me I said no to most of them because it wasn't a good fit. Sometimes it's good to weigh your options. I always said that I was willing to wait for the right people to come around that really wanted to help me move forward.

I've been advised to keep my shield down and sometimes I'm tempted to do it, but I fear over-exposure. I've always found ways to relate myself and those who I partner with to my favorite heroes. I relate to Captain America because he was always mission-driven and adamant about freedom. He always stands up for what is right and not just what other people want. I could relate because I was always treating everything like a mission. I didn't have time for games, so I was always serious. I just recently learned that I could relax and not rush. She was one of the few people that encouraged me to relax and that I didn't have to be in "conquer the world" mode all the time. Even though she has only been in my life a few months, she has done more than people who were around prior to that. This is a perfect example that sometimes people will come along and support you more than those that you have known forever. I never really saw the importance of being organized and didn't really care for lists, and that came from my young mindset. I also hated the paperwork side of business. I just wanted to be out in the field so bad that I didn't pay attention to all the legal things and taking notes.

My friend leads in the realm of being organized so I take her pointers and tips whenever she gives them. She leaves it to me to make the final decision. I can say that we have great teamwork and it is nice to have a legitimate partner. As a person that can handle myself, this is all I wanted. A person that sees that I work ridiculously hard at what I want. We may have our small disagreements, but this doesn't mean disloyalty. I think it's great that her weaknesses compliment my strengths and vice versa. A lot of people tell me I do too much or that they can't keep up so it's nice when someone comes along who can. I have always said that you must do a lot of hard work yourself to truly understand someone who does more than one thing. It gives you a sense of readability. You immediately understand what each other is passionate about. The beautiful thing is that sometimes your passions intertwine and allow you to seamlessly work together. It doesn't feel forced or awkward, but rather that you should have worked together all along. It's hard to walk away from someone like that because the energy is so perfectly matched. I won't fight for something or someone that continues to give me resistance, especially when I make it clear that I'm there to help.

I don't easily turn my back on people, but if I feel unappreciated I will. Sometimes you must go through bad partners in order to get to a great one. I have had some bad partners that didn't want to meet their end of the bargain. It sucks and I'm terrible at letting people go, but it must happen sometimes. I'm not sure if it was envy or spiteful spirits but they eventually became toxic. I guess that's what happens when people want your crown. There is no manual for how to obtain your crown and even for how to keep it. These are the things I think about as I plan my next moves while sipping

wine or a beer. Planning can sometimes be messy. Scratched out words, writing on the wall, pictures of places to visit. This is all part of the plan. It's not glamorous all the time. The behind the scenes stuff never is. Some things can't be explained to people because they won't understand it. A lot of people speculate when they don't know what you're doing. Instead of just taking your word for it, they will tell you that you're not doing anything. I don't think anyone should be

able to come along and tell you what you're not doing.

Chapter 23: Passing the Mantle

I have never been willing to give my life for anything before, but entrepreneurship is something I found to be worthy of just that. I remember when I found out my grandfather was also an entrepreneur. It made me so happy because prior to that I never knew much about him, or how he lived. I love my journey as an entrepreneur, and I am proud to keep that legacy going within my family

Knowing the different types of businesses my grandfather started was just the push I needed. I had been on the fence and this was the information that tipped me to the other side. Finding out that he had done so many different things inspired me to go the same route and do multiple things myself. He was an investor in real estate, had a non-profit, a repair shop and a construction company. I don't have many regrets in my life, but one of the few was not being able to be mentored by him before he passed. I spent time around him, but he was never much of a talker and over time I just learned to accept it. Unfortunately, that was just the type of person he was. I used to approach my mom about it and ask her why he was that way. She simply said that we are from two different eras. In his era, it was up to the grandkids to reach out to the grandparents. I questioned it a lot because I couldn't make sense of it.

After he passed, I finally found out that he did these great things, so I started to feel his presence and I also felt empowered. At that moment, it was as if he was passing me the torch. I simply nodded in agreement and took hold of it with pride and I have not put it down ever since. The whole thing happened so suddenly it was almost like a blur.

It's been said that if you aren't willing to die for something then you aren't fit to live. I share that sentiment in my heart. They will have to decapitate me before I think of quitting. One thing I respect about my grandpa is that he was always purpose-driven and he never did things that he felt was a waste of time. I honestly think that him being a Capricorn has played a strong influence in me being so legacy-driven. His birthday being two days after mine plays a big part in me refusing to let the entrepreneurship legacy die with me.

It is scary to me, knowing that currently I am the only person in my family who Is taking the entrepreneurial path. You always hear stories about people that were "the first" in their family to do things such as going to college or starting a business. I didn't know that I joined that club until I realized that I am the pioneer for entrepreneurship in my generation.

When It comes to my grandfather, I'm glad that I found out what type of man he was, even if it came after he passed. I know that he wasn't much of a talker, but I will make sure that people know him through me. Even at the speaking engagements that I attend, I always make sure to say his name. I believe that no one really dies, their spirit simply merges with you. I've always been spiritual, and I believe in an afterlife. This is the reason I do a lot of things with redetermination. I think about the future a lot more than people realize. I already know that I won't be out in the field doing sales forever so I am lining other things up for when I can't do it anymore. As of late, I have been obsessed with the concept of passing something down and I truly believe I will. This is partially why I have set the bar so high for myself. One of the best things I have learned is that we don't have as much time as we think we have. I encourage you to take care of the elders around you because one day it will be you. I didn't always see things this way, but when it finally hit me, I was shell shocked for sure.

When I'm gone, if I have kids, I want them to have something to brag about. I also want them to understand that a lot of work went into this lifestyle, and a lot of reward came out of it as well. I won't force them to do entrepreneurs if that's not what they want, but the option will be there for them as long as I'm around. I want them to have as many choices as possible since I didn't have that many. I wasn't satisfied with the limited opportunities in front of me, so I did what I do best and made my own. I have had spiritual conversations with my grandfather, and I know that he is proud of the person I have become. My feet are firmly planted on this path and will not waver.

What makes my life even easier is that I currently don't have any children, so now is the perfect time for me to do everything that I want to do. I can give 100% to my business, I can travel with ease, and I'm not weighed down with childcare expenses. I want my foundation to be as solid as possible, so all that I do is for the bigger picture. I have always said that if I ever have kids, I want them to be proud to say; "my dad is an entrepreneur". The mere thought of that happening keeps me driven. I have always been aware that children would be my outcome if there were anything that I could do greater than myself. Generational growth has always been in the back of my mind. My grandfather passed down this amazing entrepreneurial gene and I will keep it going and nod my head in agreement.

There is a sense of tradition and respect that people can feel through my energy, even at the young age of 30. As I watched my grandfather get lowered into the ground, while shedding uncontrollable tears, I realized that this was my defining moment. This is what forced me to get my life together and make better choices. It sucks that most times life forces us to "wake up" after someone else passes.
I don't have too many regrets in my life, but I still can't help wondering what type of entrepreneur I would be if I was mentored by him. I'm sure that his input would be a true guiding light. And despite him not being much of a talker, he had a heart of gold, so I'm grateful to share this quality with him.

I don't think I would be doing fragrances or books if he was still around and I'm not even sure what type of entrepreneur I'd be. He was a tough but fair man so I'm sure he would want me to at least attempt to try first. This would not be an issue because I have always preferred to take my chances with certain things.

Because I was inspired by him to carry on my entrepreneurial journey, I wanted to make a personal fragrance in his honor. I was excited to do this after coming up with one for myself simply entitled "Kayles" which was a combination of coconut and cool water. When it came to my own scent, I went with something sophisticated. My grandfather, however, was a bit more traditional so it made me wonder what he would smell like if it was contained in a fragrance. After thinking on it for a few weeks, I came to the conclusion, that he would be into earthly scents so I came up with one mixed with leather, sandalwood, and hints of mint or basil that I think he would be proud of. After all, he is the sole reason for my current endeavors, and I will never falter on them because the crown I wear was passed down from him. I follow Grandpa Eddie's path faithfully and I can feel him smiling down on me from time to time. Even though we came from two different generations, I still found a way to love my grandpa and honor him. I have a picture of him that I look at every chance I get. The picture along with his fragrance are both my way of keeping him close to me. I never realized how much my grandpa Eddie and I had in common until I forged my own path and started to apply some of his principles to my own life. One of them was to always give back which is a principle I had been following even before I had the dream of being extremely wealthy. Even though he didn't smile much, his heart shined through every time.

One of the key moments that stuck out to me on his passing was all the people that came forward and stated that he had inspired them all to start their own companies. I didn't know what companies I would start of my own, but I knew the energy from him was felt and that this was my newfound path. I am a far cry from the person I once was, and I love who I am now. I can proudly say he walks hand in hand with me and I find myself saying "what would my grandpa do?" then I sit and get still, then whatever I'm stumped on subsides and I can think clearly. This always applies when I'm frustrated and feel that my progress isn't moving fast enough. Sometimes it's best to just breathe and recompose yourself. As I found out what kind of entrepreneur he was, I use his example as a beacon within my own life.

Outside of friends calming me down, I often think of how level headed he was when making his decisions for his businesses. This is usually enough for me to get back on track when I feel lost. Because of his legacy which includes a non-profit, I am using his example to build an entrepreneurial school for the next generation. The name of this future institution will be Billionaires Under Construction. How will it look? I don't know yet, nor do I know the location, but it was an idea given to me by the universe, so I'm sure it will give me inspiration on what the blueprint for it will be. Even though it will be further down the road on my journey, I do have a general idea of the curriculum that the school would have. It would be based on things that would be useful to a child or teenager who is considering entrepreneurship

Chapter 24. Facades & Castles

"Everyone thinks that I have it all but it's so empty living behind these castle walls"

I have concluded that some people don't ask the right questions when it comes to preparation. Since we are all kings and queens in training, think of it like a castle under construction. Would you invite other people into a castle that isn't ready? You must prepare rooms. You must customize the stairs. There is a lot of inside work when developing your castle. What color do you want the bricks to be? How wide do you want it? This applies to anything. I always consider myself to be a work in progress. I'm never officially complete. Just when I think I'm officially done, something else comes along that I need to do. This is how I view my journey. I started off with choosing blue bricks for the outside. Then I made the inside steps white. I am still building my castle, but the beautiful thing is that it's mine.

This is all a metaphor for building a dream. As I build my castle and empire, I am aware that things will always come up on the road to wealth. As a billionaire under construction, I have made a personal promise to always be genuine. I have a great deal of respect for Warren Buffet, who I have learned a lot from. My castle is still being built but I do have a better idea of how I want It to look.

People only seem to notice the finished product, they never see how much work truly goes into it, especially when working from scratch. I was warned not to do it but I like a challenge, so I did it anyway. Sometimes I prefer it to be done the hard way because anything worth having is never easy. As I work to increase my net worth and become more successful, I will always be genuine. Money is simply an amplifier of who you are. I've always enjoyed helping people and I believe it will only be magnified back into my life.

It has been a long road, but I have a lot of people that are depending on me, so I can't quit, no matter how many doubtful days I have. My willpower has always been strong, but I have never felt the need to be loud about it. It's easy to succumb to what society wants you to be, but if you do that is a facade because you aren't being true to yourself and you're just being a follower. True freedom is what I call the superman effect. When I no longer worked for someone else, it was extremely liberating to the point that I felt just like superman. This made me use my time more wisely and instead of wanting to go clubbing, I stayed home and read about real estate and investing. I honestly think that I got over the club scene very quickly because I was exposed to it early in life. Once I saw that it was the same thing day in and day out, I decided to walk away. I have always despised mundane experiences. I tend to have a larger-than-life view because of my great experiences throughout life. My mom was smart enough to always expose me to different things. This is part of the reason I want the world and not just the city.

As I build my castle, I have found that I must be fiercely selective about who I let in. So, people who take it upon themselves to tell me what should be inside of my castle to be green instead of blue doesn't sit well with me. I have a very specific way that I want it to look and if there are too many "you should" responses, my response to them is "who are you?" This is only geared toward people that don't know me well and who don't take the time to do so. I am a bit of a hardhead, but I have a heart of gold. I have poured out my passion within certain people and ventures. My castle is accommodating for those that have paid their dues in my life. This is not about money because I have always been fully capable of putting in my own work towards what I want. But they have spent countless hours on the phone with me, hearing out my ideas and vice versa. I have always said that if you can work with me, and not be quick to leave when things are tough, I will make room for you.

Whether I'm halfway around the world or at home, those who are cemented will always have a spare key. I trust them with my life and it's not something I take lightly. Despite having multiple virtual friends on social media and the like, this only applies to a main core of five or so people that I speak to on a regular basis. Whether I initiate the call to them or vice versa, we know that we are there to support each other without question. These are the people that matter, and we provide each other with the opportunity of always being readily available for one another. The only people that I care to share my good news with are those that I consider to be on this level with me. They know my work ethic, and they know that I am a man of my word. We allow each other time to grow at our own paces and we support each other's virtual castle, knowing that one day it will no longer be a dream, but a true solid structure.

I tell people all the time that my dream is a work in progress. Whether or not they believe me isn't my problem. As most people in business say, the results will reveal themselves. I've gotten over the phase of being overly excited and sharing things with the public before they happen. This is sometimes hard to do when you are passionate about everything and immediately want to share it with the world. So because of past experiences, I now keep it within my circle. I don't share it with someone else unless a rapport has been built.

Chapter 25: Laying the Blueprint

Once you start to look at your life as a blueprint or foundation for someone else, you see things differently. I have gone from an "all about me" mentality to thinking more about others. The truth is, if it were just about me, I would have probably given up a long time ago. I heard a saying that I find to be true. It is an African proverb and it states;

if you want to go fast, go alone, but if you want to far then go together.

I like the "go together" method, so I have always incorporated those who are important in my life as part of my "why" when it comes to building an extraordinary life for myself. None of the amazing things I'm currently doing would be possible if I was a solo player. As the architect, I need someone else to be the painter, someone else to do construction, etc. This is known as laying the groundwork. I take my time designing, so the foundation for my structure will be as strong as possible. The end-result will be a beautiful castle, somewhere around 8,000 square feet in size, on the waterfront with beautiful decor, spiral staircases and the whole nine yards.

Having books that I've written, a fragrance line, and a wine collection are part of the foundation of my castle, but they will be stronger than the average businesses. I know that my brands will stand the test of time because of the different skilled workers that help strengthen this foundation. I love seeing other people "work their magic" when it comes to the construction of this dream castle. As the architect, I also like when people step back and watch me work, so I give them the same respect. Most likely I will have to take detours along the way when it comes to building my castle, but completely quitting is never going to be an option. I have invested too much time, energy, creativity and planning into this way of life just to be easily swayed by other people. I have absolute belief that my dreams will be fulfilled, and I will never compromise on that.

Quite often I get the inevitable question; "what if it doesn't work out?"
Honestly, I don't even entertain that question because my faith is so strong and why would I be blessed with so many great ideas if it were not meant to be? I always look at my ideas like assignments from the universe, and just like school, I never allow others to copy my work or distract me.

I'm always willing to be risky, but I take calculated risks and no longer make sporadic decisions. I'm often told that billionaires are never sloppy and as a person laying a strong foundation, I recognize that I can't be sloppy either. As I'm building this blueprint, I'm still learning as I go. I wish there was a manual on how to build a blueprint, but that would take the fun out of it. There's a thrill that comes with diving in head-first without knowing what to do and figuring it out as you go. Instead if rushing in blindly, just put one foot in front of the other and repeat the process. You will figure out the best pace later. You can't compare your chapter 6 to someone else's chapter 20 when it comes to the pace of your life. Everyone is obviously at a different phase of the process, so it's best to just run your own race. It is very easy to fall into the trap of comparing yourself to other people's progress if you're not careful. I have certainly fallen victim in the past and it sucks. You start to feel like you're behind in the race after seeing the progress that others have made.

The important thing to know is that you can't help others with an empty cup so sometimes you may have to be selfish. Focus on yourself until you get to a point where you can help other people. It can be hard to be selfish when you are a good person. Part of laying this blueprint is sometimes saying no to having fun, so you can focus on creating it.

Chapter 26. Concrete to Palm trees

"The best thing you can do is expose yourself to a better life"
D. Williams

In recent years, I've become obsessed with living a better life, mainly because I have been exposed to it more and more. I've met multi-millionaires and people who have condos or houses by the ocean. After seeing their awesome achievements, I have no interest in hanging out socially. Being in those lavish environments was not an accident, I purposely put myself in position to have these experiences. I was tired of seeing the same old places and needed a change. Anyone that knows me knows that I love variety. When something starts to feel redundant, I take it upon myself to change it.
I never want a life of regret, and seeing others live in their own terms, I felt left out. I saw them travelling to London, Brazil, Tokyo, Australia and places like the Bahamas. I immediately wanted a taste of that. A light bulb went off and I said "Hey! I want to travel and see the world too". So, I started reading books about dream vacations and exotic places.

I never wanted to drive a Lamborghini just to show-off or feel like I was better than other people. I want one because that is a car I like and want to be in. After being exposed to a better life, I don't want anything less. Coming from a concrete jungle, it took a while to get a new vision in my mind. I used to be so scared to talk about different things because the people around me were stuck in the concrete jungle mentality. They couldn't understand why I wanted something different.

I owe a debt of gratitude to those who introduced me to the laptop lifestyle and how there was more than one way to live it. I love the fact that I can board a flight or bus at any time, day or night to go wherever I needed. I still remember having to wake up at 4 a.m. to catch a bus headed to upstate New York to get out the word out about my book and I would do it all over again.
Fast forward a few years and I now have clients outside of the U.S. for fragrances and I also created a buzz in Africa for my books. I used to regret taking so long to figure this out, but now I honestly don't. I know that things had to happen in a certain way for my faith to be solidified and now it's unbreakable.

I've always heard that every overnight success story was ten years in the making. I always thought it was just something people said, until I started to achieve my own success. After that I started noticing the amount of time that it took to get where I am. I feel as if I have been able to do a lot in a small amount of time, so I often reflect on life. The TV shows and music I listened to have changed as a result of being exposed to this new life. Although, I'm often in business mode, I think it's good to take a break and wind down with some TV. Outside of watching things like Shark tank or Undercover Boss, I watch cartoons or comedy shows. YouTube has become my favorite form of television and I barely watch my own tv. I think being grounded as a kid had a lot to do with it, so now standard TV is not as important to me as it normally would be.

I'm always on the grind for my business and stopping is easier said than done. Especially if I'm unhappy with my current environment and need a change. Anytime I can, I binge watch motivational videos and mastermind about things that will contribute to my dream. Once I accomplish my goals, then maybe I will rest. Until then, I have work to do. I must admit, I sometimes put unnecessary pressure on myself because I always feel that there's more to be done. Watching TV would distract me from what's important, so I try not to take breaks. Whenever I consider slowing down, I think of Grant Cardone, Gary Vaynerchuk, Daymond John, and Mark Cuban. People like them are constantly hard at work, so why should I show down when I have some catching up to do. Most of my peers figured out their paths early and even though I didn't have the same starting point, my awakening was still right on time.

Billionaire music mogul Jay Z was 26 when he became a rapper. He also started his own record company at the same time. This wasn't necessarily be choice. He worked hard, but still could not get a traditional record deal. That motivated him to do it on his own. He had a great partner to help too, but he basically took himself from rags to riches and I admire that a great deal. I love that I can relate to his story because I considered the same path at one time, but I'm glad I found this path instead. It fits my personality perfectly and allowed me to be myself in all aspects. If I want to be outspoken and bold, I can do that. If I want to be more behind the scenes, I can do that as well.

This is the reason I have my hands in multiple ventures because I don't want to be type casted and only be known for one thing throughout my entire career. I am all about mastery, but I want to master multiple things, not just one. That's why I make it a point to study people like Jay Z and others that have been mentioned throughout this book. He mastered music, then fashion, then wine and liquor, and other ventures. I do see the importance of doing things one at a time because it always adds up in the end.

Another thing that attracted me to this lifestyle is being able to customize everything. I have been in car showrooms and played with 3D models, so I know exactly how I want my Lamborghini to be. It never gets old for me to be out in the field preparing myself for billionaire status. I'm sure there are thousands of Lamborghini pictures on the internet, but that's not my style. I like to be up close and personal with my future aspirations. Doing things that way solidifies it even more for me and motivates me to keep going. Believe it or not, I've already calculated the amount of money I will need to make this purchase. I need those numbers to always be fresh in my head because that solidifies the notion that I will have it. When I had the chance to sit behind the wheel of a Lamborghini, the experience was so surreal it almost brought me to tears. I can just imagine how it will be when I finally own one.

This is part of my transition from the concrete jungle lifestyle to a life of beaches and Palm trees. I yearn for this life, and soon enough I will have it.
As a person who likes to always be on the move, I would consider myself an eagle in comparison; venturing from country to country because my perfume line has given me clients all around the world.

Chapter 27 Black Excellence

"Black excellence, I'm going to let them see" D. Williams

Black Excellence is a concept I wasn't properly educated about when I was younger. Back then I was a little sloppy because I didn't care much for my own appearance but watching the likes of Sean Combs and Shawn Carter have shown me what black excellence is all about. Honestly, I can go on forever about the many icons that have inspired my personal and business life.
Because of people like Daymond John, I see that reaching the upper echelon in the African American community is achievable. Although his wealth and status have reached levels that would impress royalty, that makes him even more of a role model for people of color. With so many great role models, I no longer allow anyone to tell me that something can't be done. My question to them is "why not?" If a person says that, but still can't articulate a valid answer, I simply walk away. My time is now spent gaining a rank of excellence, but not to prove it to anyone except myself. The idea of making it to companies like Black Enterprise, Forbes, or Entrepreneur magazine, wasn't always my aim, but life has a way of changing things. For example; I used to go out of my way to prove things to other people, now I'm only interested in proving it to myself. Trying to prove things to other people gets old fast. Your "why" must be deeper than that. If you waste time trying to keep up with others, it never goes far because their pace is naturally different from yours. In fact, I don't blame them. It's not their job to sit around and wait for you to catch up.

To be honest, the road that led me here has been long and strenuous, but I wouldn't have It any other way. Whenever the business road gets a little bumpy, I often think of my favorite entrepreneurs and I say to myself; "What would they do?" Their blueprint always helps me find the right decision.

I have great respect for billionaires outside of the entertainment industry as well, like Kevin O Leary. His story is another one that I can relate to. He once told a story about a store he worked at in his younger days. He said one of the managers told him to get on his knees and scrape a piece of gum off the floor, and because he refused, they fired him. He said because of that situation he is now a billionaire. I feel that I relate to him in that way because my jobs of the past are what led me to where I am today. They showed me what I was willing and not willing to tolerate. The 9 to 5 routine can sometimes be demeaning, and it will either suppress your self-esteem or it will motivate you to fight your way out. I chose to fight my way out and have no regrets. Most people say that if you die while working a 9 to 5 they will replace you before your obituary is even written. The sad truth about standard jobs is that most front-line employees are considered expendable.

This is exactly what helped start me on my path. It encouraged me to be part of the next generation of black excellence. I realized that if I focused on expressing my untapped creativity and helping those around me, my life would be much more meaningful. Life is also more joyful when you block out the negative opinions of others.

Recently I've made the decision to take a step back from social media because I realized it was taking up valuable time that should have been dedicated to my business. My social media was controlling me instead of the other way around. It was at the point of interfering with my sleep. I would go to bed at 10pm and wake up again by 1am just to check social media. I didn't realize how much damage it was causing until I started crashing in the middle of the day and I've never been known to take naps like that. My goal is always to get as much done as possible and then rest at the appropriate time. These irregular sleep patterns were also impairing my decision-making skills, causing me to seek help from unqualified people. That became a valuable lesson learned.

Taking a much-needed break from social media was the best decision I ever made. It got my sleep patterns back on track and helped me focus more on what I should have been doing long ago. It was very liberating because I didn't feel so imprisoned by it anymore. Strangely enough, many people consider it taboo not to be in social media, but I no longer subscribe to popular opinion. I share whatever I choose to share in the digital world and when my "digital associates" pressure me to do more, it's an immediate turn-off since they don't know me personally.

Considering that I'm not one to be rushed, I have found that being on social media causes you to be hasteful for no reason. It also makes you compare yourself to others, which I despise because the higher you put others on a pedestal, the lower you feel about yourself.

I started my social media hiatus by doing it for 3 days, and since I liked it, I extended it to a full week. During this time, I was able to get a lot of things done like a business plan for my champagne line, paperwork printed for my dream car, found easy ways to save money, and found some great information on real estate. Because I was able to get a lot done in such a short time, I often wonder how much I could have gotten done if I took a year off from social media? I am currently working toward doing just that.

The only people who knew about my social media hiatus were those in my immediate circle. They were the only ones important enough to know how to find me. I had a conversation with a friend who despises Facebook and is notorious for going days without telling the entire world
what she is up to. At one time I would share all my information on Facebook. People knew about my relationship as well as my business moves.
That's the stigma of social media! You feel as if you must share your life events with everyone else. Why? Because it's one big competition. My friends had to reassure me that it's okay not to tell the entire world what I'm up to or who I am involved with.

I know some who have completely deleted their social media and I have the upmost respect for them. Honestly, I don't think I could do that because it has helped me build my businesses and expand my brands outside of my local area. In fact, most of my sales and support would reflect that. I remember a quote that I once heard;

"the only way to blow up is outside of your own city".

Out of all my clients, I must say, most of them have come from outside my town or city. I've had clients in California, New Jersey, Atlanta, and even the UK. I have learned to be in control of my social media, so I can go 2 to 3 days without posting anything. At one time, I couldn't go 2 to 3 hours without posting something. I felt like I had to because everyone else was constantly updating their own status. One big competition.

I no longer feel the need to compete with the success of others when I have my own to achieve. I realized I had to be my own person. I can't let other people's social media statuses define me. I find it strange that someone you have never met in person could have so much influence over your decisions. #NeverAgain

Another great discovery on black excellence for me was finding out that some of the people I networked with have made it to the Forbes "30 under 30" list. Knowing this motivated me even more and added to my goals. This also made my dreams move closer to reality now that I knew people personally that made this legendary list. Instead of being jealous or envious, their success motivated me to work harder to solidify my own brands.

The idea of one day having endorsements, multiple companies, investment stocks and island ownership have come closer to a reality for me. Especially after finding others with similar goals and being able to ask them questions and advice. Iron sharpens iron so it's always important to be around people who sharpen me. In my opinion I can't learn or grow from someone who's at the same level that I'm at. I need to be around those who have exceeded my level so I can learn how to grow like they did. I do my best to stay away from those with a "crabs-in-a-barrel" mentality. I have no interest in fighting at the bottom of the barrel. I would prefer to break the barrel so that none of us are trapped.

Life is meant to be lived beautifully, at least that's how I feel. When I think about black excellence, I think of exceedingly wealthy people who come from humble beginnings like me and do amazing things like build schools in their childhood community. True excellence is not about getting money it's about what you do with it. People who use their money in that way are the reason that I plan to build a school of my own in the future.

Sometimes you may hear wealthy people in interviews talk about having money in offshore accounts and other nuggets of information that help hungry listeners like myself. Their interviews can be quite entertaining, but I now focus on the rare nuggets of information that the average person overlooks. So much can be learned from millionaires and billionaires if you pay close attention to their content. It's amazing to find that some of them own entire islands all to themselves. How awesome would that be to have your own freaking island?

Chapter 28: The Royal Chairs

As a King, I prefer to keep my royal court as a small, tightly knit circle. Each one playing their respective role as if on a chess board; Knight, Rook, Bishop, Pawn, all surrounding and protecting the King and Queen. I love being around other kings and queens that have their own royal court and are building their own castle.

I've come a long way from doing nonsensical things to making better decisions and taking more calculated risks, while keeping a select few in my circle.
I agree with the concept that iron sharpens iron and being around people who want the best from life is infectious. I often ask myself "where have these people been?" Even though it has been 4 years since I made the life changing decision to build my own brands and become an entrepreneur, it has been an amazing ride.
I have a great deal of admiration and respect for those in my royal court, and I am not the only one that wants to be in the upper echelon and 1 percent of society. Some of those around me want millions and some want billions like myself.
Building an empire is both fun and challenging, but I no longer allow myself to get so tense about it like I used to. Sometimes it turns into a small rivalry similar Bill Gates & Warren Buffett, but at the end of the day it's all in respect.
When it comes to the journey, it doesn't matter how you start, as long as you finish. Having the right people around has greatly helped me in staying true to myself and the goals that I have personally set in place. I watch those in my royal court stick to their goals and their discipline often helps me stick to mine.

I am extremely proud of those that are on a mission to better themselves. As a billionaire under construction, I hope I continue to inspire and motivate others that come across my path. I have boldly stepped into my position with the help of others and I will forever be grateful. It brings me to tears to think about my own progress because I remember the days when I had no direction and how I would start things, but never finish them. I have been eager to redeem myself after dropping this bad habit and now is the time. I remember wanting to do 10,000 things all at once and now I'm focused on 4, so it feels like much less of a load. At one point, I didn't care how I looked or if my clothing matched, but after seeing the example of people who took pride in themselves it has certainly rubbed off on me.

Someone once said that you should dress like you own the bank, not like you need a loan from it. This comment resonated with me, so I made sure that my image portrayed good taste and savvy, hence, I now have an upgraded wardrobe which I am proud of.

When I was told not to care about what others think, I took it the wrong way. I felt that it meant not caring about absolutely anything. The fact is you must simply find balance. These days, I finally see what awaits me on the other side of success and the beautiful part is, no one can take it away from me. Your success rests on your shoulders and no one else's. It feels so fucking awesome to be in a league of my own. I can now stand with the people that have done things that are larger than life. There is absolutely no shame in admitting that you like nice things and I know I damn sure do. I used to always say that my Lamborghini is waiting for me. It felt good to say that because it put me in the mind frame of those who already have one. Success is on the other side of fear and the more you contemplate how scary it looks, the further away it gets. The fact is that your imagination works on an entirely different level than what's truly in front of you. That's the beauty of the law of attraction; your mind controls the circumstances. So, if you look at something greater or smaller than what it already is, then that's what it will be. Why? Because perception is reality. My advice to you is stop fucking procrastinating. Go get that Bentley. Go get that mansion or estate. Go travel the entire world if you choose. On second thought, don't just choose one, go after them all. I used to wait for the "perfect time" to do things until I realized there was no such thing. If you want to become a billionaire or millionaire, just go for it. Waiting on people to give you permission to get what is already yours and has your name on it will only lead you to disappointment. Never let other people dictate how your life goes. When you truly make decisions, no matter the outcome, you won't regret it.

The great part about my journey has been my ability to express myself and my creativity freely, because that's what I needed most. I urge you to get a taste of pure freedom and fight for it. Stick up your middle finger to anyone who tries to stop you or change your dream. If someone tells you that what you're about to do is crazy, just remember, its only crazy until you do it. So, be fucking crazy and think as big and outrageous as you want. Don't let people with no ambition talk you out of anything. Life is your stage, so make it a grand one.

I have absolutely no regrets from the choices that I made. I live my life my way and I encourage you to live your life by your design. Write your own script and never give anyone else the pen. If people don't get your vision, that is not your problem. So, don't stress yourself out trying to force people to understand your vision who may not even care to listen to it.

Even though I was slow to take risks, I encourage you to take as many fucking risks as you can. The fact is, no one is going to come save you and push you on to the path of your dreams. I personally have told myself I'm leaving this earth on an empty tank and that whatever businesses I am guided to start, I will.

No matter where I am on my journey there are a set of chairs around me that are solidified for those who meet my five-year rule. If you are consistently supportive throughout that time and your personality compliments mine, then there is a seat with your name on it. Anyone who is solidified at this table with me keeps me inspired. The great part is, even though they may be on a different path, each of us are still going in the same direction. There's a quote that always rings true for me and that is; *"You will never hear complaints from those doing more than you"*. People who fit that category will always have a special place in my heart.

Chapter 29: Knighted

"Alright kid, you're an entrepreneur now" D. Williams

I have always entertained the idea of passing my businesses down to my children whenever that time comes. I have watched plenty of movies where a king, on his deathbed, decides to pass down the kingdom and rulership to his son or daughter. There are so many examples of this happening, even in The Lion King when Mufasa said to Simba;

"The sun will set on my time here and will rise with you as the new king".

The fact that I don't have any children is a sign that now is the time for me to grab the bull by the horns and spread my brands all around the world. By the time any children get here I want them to have choices I didn't have. If and when I do have children, I want the castle and throne to be solidified for them.
Anything in my legacy, whether it's the wine collection, the perfume line, the books, or even the future hotel business, I'll be excited to hand over the keys to the kingdom when that time comes. I'll make them earn it of course with a little sweat equity, but ultimately the kingdom will be theirs at the end of the day. I can't predict if, and when I will have children, but it is something I think about quite often as I build my empire. It always excites me to think of them one day proudly saying; "My father has multiple businesses".
Sure, that would be an awesome conversation for me to witness, but even more, I want them to own land. A legacy of ownership is even more important than money. The fact is, money comes and goes, but land is a lot harder to take away. I would be proud to show them how to handle the kingdom and not abandon them at the first sign of trouble. I want them to look at my wealth as inspiration not privilege. I want them to be inspired at the level of Les Brown, who said;

"Shoot for the moon because even if you miss, you'll land among the stars"

If you have passion for something it can be felt through all barriers. I have been told that my passion for business can be felt, even when communicating with someone through the computer screen. I would hope that my children inherit the same passion I have, instead of trying to force it on them. I chose this life and I will give them the same respect to choose what they want. I'm happy to be a financial cushion for them once I see that they are serious about their path. I would also make sure that they are able to have an earlier start than I did.

It sometimes brings me to tears when I think of how far my life has come. It gives me such a sense of pride, knowing that both my businesses and wealth are the fruits of my labor. Nothing was simply handed to me, I had to earn it, so my children will work for theirs as well. I love the idea of generational wealth and how it has changed my thinking. When I look back at the financial level I started at, I have no intention in going back.

Sometimes I wonder if I should tell my kids about my wealth when they're still young? I often look for tips from others in that area since it is new to me. Ultimately, I think it's up to the individual to discuss that with their children or not. Honestly, I probably would because that's just how my personality is.

I often joke with people by saying that I'm scared to have kids because they would probably be hardheaded like me. This is a running joke among friends, but I'm sure my kids will inherit some of my traits. Even if they are hardheaded just like me, I would love them just the same. I'm sure that my stubborn ways gave my mom a run for her money, so I'm preparing myself, in case my children are the same way.

Another running joke among my friends is that I'm a father in training since many of them have their own kids for me to train with. For the most part, I have received their blessings in the area of fatherhood. It makes me laugh whenever they tell me stories about their kids being disobedient. Ironically, it never deters me from wanting to start a family, in fact, it makes me want kids even more. Something about looking in their tiny faces and saying "this is all for you" is both emotional and humbling. I have always had a soft spot for kids, so I'm eager to go through that experience.

As a billionaire under construction, I've often heard the phrase; it is not about you. What does that statement mean? Well, everyone has a "why", which explains the reason they are doing whatever project or business they're doing. The problem is, when you make your "why" about you, it never goes very far. When the weight of a situation if on us we tend to let ourselves down, but if someone else depends on us we tend to do whatever it takes to make it happen. It doesn't necessarily have to be family to motivate you. Your "why" can be friends as well, but I find that your own children are the greatest reason to do anything.

I look at myself as a work in progress since I don't have children, so I use my nieces, nephews and younger cousins as a form of inspiration for me to push forward.

Since I'm already a natural family man, I began to study lions and their families. I apply the same tactics they use in the wild when caring and protecting for my own family. Lions are never sporadic they are very calculated in how they move and attack. The amazing thing is that it doesn't matter the color of the lion; whether black, yellow or white, they are all aggressive when it comes to their family. One of the key things I was taught is that if you take care of family in times of need, they will take care of you in your time of need. I will make sure to teach my children this same value as they grow. I am often told that sometimes I think too far ahead but I love doing it. I like to think ahead because my family always did the same thing. They had high hopes and expected great things from me so I would expect the same from my children. Since learning about universal laws like attraction, I will speak nothing other than positive things into their life.

When I was younger, we travelled a lot to places like Florida, Washington D.C. etc. Traveling ended up becoming a yearly tradition for my family and I'm so excited to share those same experiences with my own children. The thought of taking international trips with them to places like Greece, the United Kingdom or the Cayman Islands amazes me. It doesn't even matter if my children are adopted or biological, I would still treat them the same. I would love to introduce them to the lifestyle of rooftop pools, balconies overlooking city skylines, and homes with therapeutic in-ground pools. I want them to see that I own important things like real estate, multiple companies, and even my own island.

Although I had a late start in the arena of entrepreneurship, they will have a head-start. I'm sure they will have rough patches, but life is not supposed to be perfect. As they say, pain is only temporary.

About the author

David Williams is a 31-year-old entrepreneur from Queens, NY. He is a two-time author and President of Kayles Fragrances. He is also the Founder of Blissful Memories by Kayles, which is his exclusive wine brand. He is also a successful speaker. Watching the success of his first book is what has motivated him to keep writing. His first book; An eagle eye with a lion's heart: How introverts can break through barriers has been his most successful book so far. He is extremely humbled by how many people can relate to what he writes about. As an aspiring billionaire, he studies the likes of Mark Cuban, Sean "Diddy" Combs, Shawn "Jay-Z" Carter and Warren Buffett. To get in contact with him, he can be found on Facebook at David Kayles Williams. His email is **wdavid447@gmail.com**

Other titles by David K. Williams

1. An Eagle Eye With Lion's Heart: How Introverts Can Break Through Barriers

2. Lions & Wolves: The Difference Between Entrepreneurs and Network Marketers

Ways to connect with David Williams
Instagram: Kaylesenterprises
Facebook: Kayles Fragrances LLC
Twitter: KaylesFragrancellc

Made in the USA
Middletown, DE
01 June 2023